Maida L. Riggs
Scholar
University of Massachusetts
Amherst

Patt Dodds
Instructional Designer
University of Massachusetts
Amherst

David Zuccalo
Practitioner
University of Massachusetts
Amherst

Early Childhood

BASIC STUFF SERIES II

7

Copyright © 1981

American Alliance for Health,
Physical Education, Recreation and Dance
1900 Association Drive, Reston, VA 22091

Stock Number: 245-26840

A Project of the
National Association for Sport and Physical Education
An Association of the
American Alliance for Health, Physical Education,
Recreation and Dance

"BASIC STUFF" SERIES

A collection of booklets presenting concepts, principles, and developmental ideas extracted from the body of knowledge for physical education and sport. Each booklet is intended for use by undergraduate majors and practitioners in physical education.

"BASIC STUFF" SERIES

Series One **Informational Booklets**
Exercise Physiology
Kinesiology
Motor Learning
Psycho-Social Aspects of Physical Education
Humanities in Physical Education
Motor Development

Series Two **Learning Experience Booklets**
Early Childhood
Childhood
Adolescence

Editorial Committee

Marian E. Kneer, *Editor*
University of Illinois,
Chicago Circle

Linda L. Bain
University of Houston

Norma J. Carr
SUNY,
College of Cortland,
New York

Don Hellison
Portland State University

Mary Kazlusky
SUNY,
College of Cortland,
New York

Barbara Lockhart
Temple University,
Philadelphia, Pennsylvania

Jack Razor
Illinois State University,
Normal

Sandra Wilbur
Tenafly Public Schools,
New York

preface

The information explosion has hit physical education. Researchers are discovering new links between exercise and human physiology. Others are investigating neurological aspects of motor control. Using computer simulation and other sophisticated techniques, biomechanics researchers are finding new ways to analyze human movement. As a result of renewed interest in social, cultural, and psychological aspects of movement, a vast, highly specialized body of knowledge has emerged.

Many physical education teachers want to use and apply information particularly relevant to their teaching. It is not an easy task. The quantity of research alone would require a dawn to dusk reading schedule. The specialized nature of the research tends to make it difficult for a layperson to comprehend fully. And finally, little work has been directed toward applying the research to the more practical concerns of teachers in the field. Thus the burgeoning body of information available to researchers and academicians has had little impact on physical education programs in the field.

The Basic Stuff series is the culmination of the National Association for Sport and Physical Education efforts to confront this problem. An attempt was made to identify basic knowledge relevant to physical education programs and to present that knowledge in a useful, readable format. The series is not concerned with physical education curriculum design, but the "basic stuff" concepts are common core information pervading any physical education course of study.

The selection of knowledge for inclusion in the series was based upon its relevance to students in physical education programs. Several common student motives or purposes for participation were identified: health (feeling good), appearance (looking good), achievement (doing better), social (getting along), aesthetic (turning on), and coping with the environment (surviving). Concepts were then selected which provided information useful to students in accomplishing these purposes.

The Basic Stuff project includes two types of booklets. Series I is designed for use by preservice and inservice teachers and consists of six pamphlets concerning disciplinary areas: exercise physiology, kinesiology, motor development and motor learning, social/psychological aspects of movement, and movement in the humanities (art, history, philosophy). This first series summarizes information on student purposes. Series II is also designed for use by teachers but with a different focus. Three handbooks are included: early childhood; childhood; adolescence. Each describes examples of instructional activities which could be used to teach appropriate physical education concepts to each age group.

The development of the Basic Stuff series has been a cooperative effort of teams of scholars and public school teachers. Scholars provided the expertise in the content areas and in the development of instructional materials. Public school teachers identified relevance to students, field tested instructional activities, and encouraged the scholars to write for general understanding.

The format of the booklets was designed to be fun and readable. Series I is structured as a question and answer dialogue between students and a teacher. Series II continues this emphasis with the infusion of knowledge into the world of physical education instructional programs. Our hope is that the Basic Stuff series can help to make this scenario a reality.

Linda L. Bain, *Editorial Committee*
University of Houston

table of contents

introduction

This booklet is one of three in the Basic Stuff Series II designed to address teachers, parents, and other adults who may be responsible for implementing physical education programs for children. This particular booklet is for children in the 2½-8 year-old age range. This introduction explains the format used to present the content in the following chapters, focuses on some critical concerns related to the teaching *process,* and draws attention to some basic ideas about curriculum building which can help you set up the best program for the youngsters with whom you work.

Format of Chapters

Chapters and Their Contents

The chapter contents of this Series II booklet follow the same headings as in Series I. You'll find information about Feeling Good, Looking Good, Doing Better, Getting Along, Turning On, and Surviving, each in its own chapter in Series II for the age group to which the booklet is pointed. Under each of these chapter headings are placed all of the concepts appropriate for the youngest age group (ranging from 2½ to 8) selected from all of the Series I booklets. Thus in this Series II booklet chapter for Feeling Good, concepts from Exercise Physiology, Kinesiology, Motor Development, Motor Learning, Psycho-Social Aspects of Physical Education, and Humanities are found, all of which relate to helping young children Feel Good in and through their movement activities.

The last part of this booklet provides Recommended Readings to help you locate additional resources to consult for ideas about further learning experiences for children beyond the scope of this booklet. Our text is designed to provide you with a framework or mindset as an access tool for making sense from the much more comprehensive activity texts and books available. Its purpose is also to give you some rational, logical criteria on which to base your own choices of specific activities taken from these other sources to incorporate into a lesson.

As an illustration, suppose you wanted to choose good running activities to help the children you instruct to improve their cardiorespiratory fitness. You also realize that the activities selected should provide maximum activity per unit of time for the largest number of children at the same time. Given these goals you find several texts suggesting either tag games or relays for developing running skills. You would probably choose a tag game over a relay, since all children could be moving at the same time rather than standing in a line waiting their turns while a few moved at once. This choice would better serve your intention for that lesson of working on the cardiorespiratory fitness of those children.

Each resource included in our Recommended Readings is annotated briefly to give you an idea of its values and strengths to use in your own teaching. In the rhythms and dance references you'll find suggestions for music and musical accompaniments as well as activities. The games and sports sources also include recommendations for equipment and apparatus. Each book on the list provides additional recommendations for resources so that you can never run out of information!

How the Chapters Are Arranged

In each of the following chapters, the format is standardized as shown below:

Concept:

The question appears in bold type in the margin

Concept presentation with questions. At the top of the page, the selected *concept* is presented, along with some related *questions* which children might ask about the concept. For instance, here are three concepts and their related questions:

1. (Doing Better) COMPARING WITH OTHERS: How can I move like others? How can others move like me? How can I move differently from others? How can others move differently from me?
2. (Coping) THE GOAL FOR THE SKILL DETERMINES THE FORM OF THE SKILL: How does my purpose affect how I do the movement?
3. (Turning On) THE JOY OF EXPERIENCING MOVEMENT: How can I move and what can I do that gives me pleasure in moving?

Learning experiences. Next you will find several suggested *learning experiences* to illustrate the particular concept. We have attempted to represent possibilities from the three broad activity areas of a well-rounded movement curriculum: games and sports; gymnastics and body control activities; rhythms and dance. We believe it is important for children to have opportunities for all of these varied experiences. The inclusion of all three activity areas in a physical education curriculum promotes well-rounded movement skill acquisition by children. Aquatics is also an important activity; however, the writing team did not consider it within the purview of this particular Basic Stuff series.

In *games and sport-related activities,* children have a chance to move in cooperative/competitive situations governed by specific playing rules. However for the younger children a category entitled *manipulative activities* might be more applicable than games, since the children will not be engaged in formal games of lower organization until they reach the age group of 6-8. Children have to learn to handle objects with some degree of success before they engage in games based on the skills of object handling. Very young children's games are more informal and usually fall into the category of free play.

Body control and gymnastics skills such as balancing, inverting, locomotion, axial/non-locomotion, and manipulative actions — the application of these fundamental skills in more specialized contexts of sports and games, dance, or gymnastics comes during subsequent periods of their lives (for example, dribbling a basketball, putting a shot, passing a volleyball). Some 7- and 8-year-olds may be very highly skilled (in the sense of a high level of performance accuracy, consistency, speed, or form) in a few isolated skills such as doing a cartwheel or pitching a baseball or passing a football, but they do not maintain this high performance level consistently across a large number of diverse skills.

In *rhythm and dance activities,* children learn to move in relation to external stimuli, usually auditory, sometimes visual or kinesthetic. Once they have acquired reasonable control over locomotion and non-locomotion patterns, they can then use them in the more restricted context of actions in a specific time frame: "run in time with the drum sounds I make," "skip in time to this piece of bouncy music." Less teacher-structured dancing may be in the form of child-created individual responses to things they *see* or *feel:* "move like a rainbow at the end of a storm," "how would you move as softly as the fur feels?"

Free Play is a special category of activity in which teachers do not structure the actions for children but allow them to make decisions about what they will do, with whom they will do it, and what equipment they wish to attempt. In this handbook there will be no special section for free play under each concept but teachers are encouraged to bear in mind that relatively substantial amounts of time for children to experiment with their growing skills "on their own" is essential for 2½ to 8 year-olds, and that free play time is a way to provide for this.

How Teachers May Use These Activities. The teacher's approach to a learning experience is probably far more important than the selection of the activity itself in determining which concepts, psychomotor skills, and attitudes children learn. For this reason there is a section for each concept that offers suggestions on how teachers might act during a lesson or activity period. To illustrate, a teacher may perform any of the following functions:

ask	observe
prompt	tell
promote	aid
bolster	suggest
choose	praise
watch	uphold
assist	query
touch	note
request	challenge
question	support
reinforce	hold
select	

How Children May Respond. The final section of our format presents possibilities for various responses from children. Just as teachers may assume functions appropriate to certain goals for activities, so may children demonstrate their awareness of concepts, physical skill levels, or attitude changes in alternative ways. Children's responses give teachers valuable information which may be used as one form of evaluation for the planned lesson, or of the children themselves. Here is a partial list of expected responses of children:

show a way	demonstrate
find a way	act
choose	describe
cooperate	select
explain	tell
experiment	try
draw	point
gesture	attempt
paint	

Discussion

Age Level Subdivisions

The members of this writing team believe very strongly that 2½ year-olds and 8 year-olds are considerably different from each other. Two and a half year-olds are not challenged by the same tasks as eight year-olds, do not respond in the same way to particular pieces of equipment, follow different social interaction systems and have different feelings of groupness, react differently to success and failure, and in essence, inhabit whole different physical, mental, social, and psychological worlds. Their capabilities are radically different, and their perceptual and motor systems are at different stages of development.

Types of Space

In developing learning activities as examples of what might be done with each concept, this writing team realized that no two environments for gross motor activities are the same. Particularly at the preschool level, and in many cases for the primary elementary grades K-3, spaces may be available with widely disparate characteristics: outdoor playground areas (with or without various types of large equipment or apparatus); indoor gymnasium spaces (usually well-equipped for games and play activities, but not for dance or gymnastics, track and field, etc.); a small-or medium-sized ordinary room with no special equipment at all, or equipment that has to be moved in or out to make a space for movement.

Each type of movement environment places certain constraints on the teacher's choice of activities for children. For example, the size of the area may dictate grouped activities rather than an individualized approach. Built-in obstacles of some sort, e.g., cabinets and bookshelves, may preclude selection of highly vigorous activities for that space.

Activity Appropriateness for Several Concepts

We have attempted to select the most relevant concepts about movement for presentation to the 2½ to 8 year-old age groups from the Basic Stuff Series I booklets, realizing that what may be appropriate and plausible for the 2½ year-old may not, in all likelihood, meet the needs of the 8 year-old. As we chose the concepts related to Physiology of Exercise, Kinesiology, Motor Development, Motor Learning, Humanities, and Psycho-Social Aspects of Physical Education, we found that the learning experiences envisioned did not fall neatly under single concepts only. Instead one learning experience could appropriately illustrate several concepts, *depending on how the teacher designed and implemented that learning experience.* For this reason, we have indicated a focus for each concept to assist the reader. If, for instance, the concept was "PERSONAL PROGRESS. How can I change my movement?" (Doing Better), the focus for the learning experiences could be "to increase success and to discover a child s own unique variations." The focus of the teacher will depend on the concept selected for presentation to the children. A focus on the benefits of participation (Why do I like to move? What are the health benefits?) might set up a series of teacher questions designed for children to answer verbally about how movement feels when running, jumping, etc. An alternative emphasis on these locomotor patterns as a basis for successful participation in more specialized forms of movement (games and sports, rhythms and dance, body control activities and gymnastics) may find the teacher challenging children to find ways of running faster, jumping farther, or leaping higher.

Teacher Responsibilities

There are three major duties for teachers to discharge:

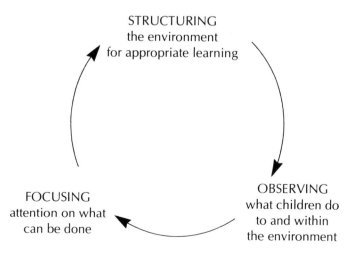

STRUCTURING
the environment
for appropriate learning

OBSERVING
what children do
to and within
the environment

FOCUSING
attention on what
can be done

Structure of the Environment

There are three dimensions to the STRUCTURE of the environment: *physical,* what objects are set out; *intellectual,* what questioning/prompting skills are used, decisions made, goals selected and by whom; *emotional,* what supporting, reinforcing, challenging expertise is provided and control demonstrated.

Physical. Structuring the physical environment means establishing the widest possible selection of gymnastic or manipulative equipment to meet the needs of the age group under supervision. There needs to be something familiar and something novel within each day's setup to create an environment which is both secure but yet offers a challenge for new learning.

Intellectual. The intellectual structure of the environment involves utilizing the "right mix" of questioning, task-setting, and suggests possibilities to children for their movement experiences. Such structure also includes conscious teacher decisions about who will make what kinds of choices during activity lessons and who sets which kinds of goals for performance.

Cognitive Responses from Children. Children's memories operate mainly as motor memories in the early stages of childhood—action rather than reaction. In Piaget's terms, the children are functioning "pre-operationally," being bound to direct experience for gathering information and thus for learning. The child's thinking process is heavily dependent on a sensory base using experiences with concrete forms: feeling different textures; tossing different-sized balls; seeing various objects fall; etc. This sensory-motor base changes to incorporate a psychological-cognitive component as children increase the complexities of their experiences with the world and concurrently their ability to make simple abstract generalizations about those experiences. According to Piaget, the crucial element underlying what is learned is what the child has selected to attend, in other words the "cues" within the experience. It becomes very important, then, for teachers to frequently use word cues and labels to help children in these younger age groups (2½-8) establish the verbal-psychological base to join with their sensory-motor base.

Complex thinking, including the development of both cognitive and affective meaning, is achieved through planned instruction to elicit experimentation and vigorous interaction with the environment. Skill in concept formation is closely linked to language acquisition, so the development of a vocabulary of movement is imperative for young children, just as development of a cognitive language vocabulary is crucial. Between five and seven years there is a major improvement in the ability to think with concepts alone (without specific reference to concrete objects of experiences), and the teacher's careful, consistent, and frequent use of labels and language during lessons can help children formulate their vocabularies in both senses.

Varying Children's Responses. Teachers have several flexible alternatives for structuring learning activities to vary children's response modes. The advantages of doing this are two-fold. First, multiple responses increase the chances of children really practicing sufficiently and showing what they can do, and second, the teacher has more varied data upon which to make judgments about children's progress and improvement in movement skills.

Teachers can plan for children to respond to tasks by *doing,* by *telling,* or by *making a permanent representation* (a painting, drawing, or sculpture). Teachers can select a single response mode for each task presented to children, or use multiple response modes concurrently to draw out several possible reactions to the same task. To illustrate, children may create a dance pattern to represent how they feel about autumn leaves falling from trees; they might describe in words how the dance pattern felt as they moved or how the leaves looked as they fell; they could draw or paint a picture to illustrate their movement patterns or the leaves actually falling.

Decision-making: Teacher and Child. One step in moving toward children's independent decision-making could be for teacher and children to jointly decide on goals with specific standards of performance, the teacher establishing who meets the goals and when. Following this step might be joint teacher-child goal setting and joint teacher-child decisions about when the goals are met, with the children's contributions including learning to measure themselves and each other to evaluate progress. Completing the move toward child independence, the teacher could shift to children individually setting their own goals and then deciding when they each meet the standards of the goal, thus gradually helping them learn how to make appropriate decisions, rather than simply allowing children to make many choices very suddenly without any sort of step-by-step plan for learning the *process* of choosing wisely.

Children's goals/Teachers' goals. Teachers cannot assume that their goals are necessarily the same as those held by the children for a given movement learning experience, particularly for the 2½-8 year-old. For example the *teacher* may plan an activity with the intention of increasing cardiorespiratory capacities, while the *child's* goal is simply to feel good while moving fast. Realizing that the teacher and children involved in a lesson all have individual personal goals within the same situation may help a teacher think about a lesson from several perspectives during the planning stages. This capacity for "multiple thinking" can enhance teacher flexibility and bring about a greater congruence between teacher's and children's expectations of final outcomes of a lesson.

Climate of Control: direct teaching or skilled nonintervention? The teacher's primary responsibility of being "in charge" may take any form from very direct control of children and environment at all times to a seemingly complete non-intervention. When a teacher is in direct control, he starts or stops all children as a group at the same time, gives specific tasks with little room for children's judgment or choices, and generally interacts with the whole group throughout the lesson rather than attending to individuals. At the non-intervention end of the continuum, a teacher may only plan the arrangement of the environment so that during the lesson itself children interact primarily with equipment or apparatus with minimal verbal prompting from the teacher. Each child chooses where, what, and with whom to move, starts and stops himself at will, and is more independent from the teacher than in the direct control situation.

For younger children, the skilled non-intervention teacher role is often more appropriate, while older children may respond equally well to either direct or indirect teacher actions. Of course there are situations for any age group which will require the whole continuum of teacher behaviors.

Teacher Flexibility. There are times when, from one lesson to another, or during a single lesson, the teacher's role will vary from direct intervention to non-intervention. Achieving such flexibility would seem to be a worthwhile goal for a teacher because it expands his repertoire of total teaching skills. As the teaching role changes, so does that of the learners, particularly with regard to decision-making. As the teacher makes fewer spontaneous choices for the whole class, individual children are free to take over that choice-making for themselves. It is important to remember that teachers need to prepare children to take responsibility for their own learning by giving them freedom to make their own choices very gradually.

Teacher as Prompter. Teaching young children requires clarity, brevity, and specificity of tasks, of questions, and of explanations. Ask a single question, and then permit children to move or respond verbally. Make one short explanation, and then repeat, if necessary, after the movement or verbal response. The responses children make to these questions, tasks, and explanations will show a gradual change with age from primarily motor responses (showing) to a combination which includes verbal ones (telling) as well. One of the teacher's major functions is to help children develop a vocabulary which will permit them to say *how* they can move, *why* they move, and how they can move *better*. It is crucial that the teacher use words to describe equipment, actions, feelings, and attitudes, and encourage the children to do likewise as they participate in activities.

Emotional. Structuring the movement environment in an emotional sense refers to the teacher's responsibility to maximize success and feelings of satisfaction for all children. Providing verbal and physical support and reinforcement for achieving goals or trying hard, or encouragement to try again and again are important teacher functions in an early childhood physical education setting.

Observing Children in the Environment

Observing what children do means seeing the details of the skills they perform and how they are performed. Observation is part of evaluation; in fact, it may be the only way young children's progress is measured. Thus it requires very astute perceptions, not only of *what* they do but of the *emotions* shown while doing it. Children's emotions are the window to the way they feel about activity, and how they feel is crucial to their total development. Only by observing what children do can you prepare the next learning step, and only by accepting and respecting children where they are, helping them feel good about what they do, and that they do not have to live up to the expectations of others, can you help them change. Older children think in terms which permit them to understand that they can improve a skill by practice, but because adults are "cognitive aliens" to the way young children think, they need to feel that they are respected for what they do and how they perform. They need to be accepted for wanting to climb. They may need to be shown that, in order to be safe, they need to be able to put two hands on a rung. Being psychologically safe is of utmost importance to skill development, for safety impels children toward further development: "try to put your thumb around the rung when you climb the ladder." Rungs must be small and close enough together to insure that this is possible. Teachers must observe that the thumb is or is not around. Children must be helped, not belittled, into putting the thumb around.

Observation, evaluation, and focus on children five and older involves three other dimensions:

1. *Did* they perform a specific task? Yes? No?
   Task: Find a way to get over a line by taking your weight on your hands.
2. *How* did they perform the task (quantitative)?
   Possible solutions for six year-olds: Bunny Hop, cartwheel, round-off, and walking on hands.
3. *What* was the quality of the movement?
   Was the cartwheel rhythmical and was the body stretched?

After each of these questions the teacher/children find ways to increase the number of children who comprehend and complete the task, the number who can perform each of the variety of ways, and the quality of the performance of each way.

Teachers can make daily notes (anecdotal records) about the progress or new achievements of each child, can use more formalized testing processes (can a child perform a particular task? how far can a child throw? how fast can a child run?), or can use informal scales to rate a child's performance. A five-step semantic differential rating may be anchored in contrasting pairs of words and the teacher marks an X somewhere between the two words to describe the child, e.g.,

	1	2	3	4	5	
timid				X		adventurous
poor sense of balance			X			good balance
makes little effort				X		tries hard
disturbs class				X		socially well-adjusted

Focusing

The focus is directed toward what can be done to support, improve, enhance, and develop emerging skills. That is really a two-way street with the teacher focusing on what the child is doing and helping children to realize what they are doing.

Focusing on what children are doing, which may be very different from what teachers expect them to do, permits on-the-spot selection of what can be done safely right now, and what needs to be done tomorrow or next week to insure appropriate planning for the next learning step. The teacher's skills of questioning/prompting need to be very carefully thought out and professionally used. Open-ended questions are more successful with younger children and, as the skills of older children become more refined and their cognitive abilities develop, more specific questions may be asked: "Can you find a way other than the cartwheel to take your weight on your hands?"

Teachers' Curriculum Design Tasks

The teacher's role is crucial in selecting, planning for, presenting, and evaluating learning activities which foster the assimilation of concepts about movement. All teachers have several tasks to accomplish: becoming aware of and developing an understanding for the *content* of physical education; *selecting* appropriate content based on the needs of the children with whom they work; *sequencing* the content and fitting it together in meaningful patterns; *planning* specifically for each separate lesson; *presenting* the content and *interacting* with the children during the lesson; *evaluating* both children's individual performances and previous lessons as a vital part of the ongoing process of continuous, progressive planning and doing.

Teachers may approach these common tasks in different ways because they are individual people who don't all think alike, because there are limitations of facilities, equipment, and other environmental resources, or because they have planned to reach specific educational objectives. Just as we suggested some general principles to consider when deciding upon appropriate teacher roles to play during lessons, we have some ideas we'd like to share with you about ways to structure a curriculum of physical activities for 2½-8 year-old children, a set of guidelines applicable in a variety of situations.

Safety First! Clothing and bare feet; equipment check pre-class; equipment setup; appropriateness of tasks.

Balance Activities' Energy Demands. Remembering from motor development that all body systems do not necessarily develop to the same degree at the same time, teachers should think carefully about planning a balance of activities with different energy demands. Quiet movement experiences should be alternated with very vigorous ones, and some periods of total rest should occasionally occur. The relative amounts of time spent across the 2½-8 age range will change. The 2½ year-olds need to rest more frequently and to change fairly often from strenuous activities to quieter ones. Rest and quiet learning experiences can decrease gradually as age increases, until 8 year-olds are moving vigorously most of the time. Not every child has to rest at the same time during an activity especially if the teacher sets up the expectation that it's "all right" to take a few moments to rest on your own and then rejoin an interesting activity group.

It is also important for teachers to realize that *conscious relaxation* is very definitely a skill that helps children learn, and should be included in your movement curriculum. Learning first to recognize tension and then to loosen or relax muscles in various parts of the body becomes not only a "here and now, look I can do it" skill for youngsters, but a long-term preventive measure and a built-in positive way to handle stress later in life.

Balance of activities with regard to energy level demands should occur within a *single* lesson, within a *series* of lessons based on the same movement theme, and across *longer* time spans such as a school year, or even several school years. Careful attention to this balance can help assure teachers that they are providing activities in accordance with the concepts of exercise physiology as well as motor development.

Balance Types of Activities. A second kind of balance should be central in a teacher's planning skills: balancing the *content,* or variety of activities taught. We've already mentioned reasons for including games and sports, gymnastics and body control activities, rhythms and dance, and free play. Free play is a particularly important aspect of the movement curriculum for this age range, and should be specifically planned as teachers are considering the content balance in their programs. Too often teachers think that every moment of an activity period ought to be pre-programmed. We too seldom realize that children need some time to be spontaneous, to create their own movement curriculum, and to design their own "off the cuff" practice experiences to integrate what has been learned — in short, to PLAY. Adult structuring may be required only to the extent of setting aside time for play, with no other restrictions on the children.

Ways to Challenge Children To Do Better. When building a curriculum of movement activities, teachers who want to challenge children to do their very best can gradually increase the *complexity,* the *duration,* the *frequency,* or the *difficulty level* of tasks. *Children should be stretched to the limits of their ever-expanding capabilities without being overwhelmed by the demands of a movement activity.*

An example of making tasks more *complex* could be practicing kicking skills alone, practicing *with* a partner to send a ball back and forth, working *against* a partner in keep-away, and trying to play two-on-two, then three-on-three, etc. This situation presents gradually increasing social interaction complexities for children to meet. Asking children to remember a single task (move in one direction), then two tasks in combination (first run and then jump), then three or more tasks (move at two different levels while changing directions at least once) is another way to increase task complexity. Still a third way to make tasks more complex is to require different responses to different stimuli ("move *fast* when you hear the bell, but *slowly* when you hear the drum").

Duration can be increased simply by spending more time on successive attempts at performing the movement task: running hard for 30 seconds on Monday and Tuesday, for one minute the next two days, and for a minute and a half on Friday.

Frequency increases are illustrated when children are asked to do as many "good" sit-ups as they can on one day, to try to do more the next day, more the next, and so on. Another possibility is to request more repetitions within a given time limit: "How many jumps over the rope can you do in 30 seconds today (how many in 30 seconds the next day? is this more than yesterday? can you try for even more tomorrow?").

Increased *difficulty* of a task may mean a change in body position — holding a balance on tiptoes rather than on the whole foot, or walking a narrower balance beam or one on an incline rather than a level beam.

Ways to Plan Variety in Your Lessons (Laban's Model). Another offering we would make to you under the umbrella of curriculum-building strategies is a very strong recommendation to fully investigate the model provided by Laban's analysis of movement for consciously varying dimensions of movement activities. His four central concepts of SPACE (where the body moves), TIME (how quickly the body moves), FORCE (with how much effort the body moves), and FLOW (with how much control and smoothness the body moves) all have, within themselves or in combinations with the others, almost limitless possibilities for flexibility and variation in lesson planning.

Of course we don't expect you to be an expert in applying Laban's concepts about movement. If you decide that his ideas are worth investigating further, some of the resources listed in Recommended Readings at the end of the booklet give a full explanation of concepts, terminology, and examples needed for applying his concepts in teaching-learning situations.

Teacher as Ongoing Curriculum Designer. The last point the writing team would like to make is that *your own* work in the teacher's role of curriculum builder and lesson planner is perhaps the ultimate test of the value of this series. We can help you get *ready* for that work in several ways, but it's up to YOU to go beyond any suggestions provided here to become truly self-directed in curriculum planning actions.

In the following chapters you'll find specific examples of activities or movement patterns appropriate for various environmental contexts and for the subject matter contexts of games and sports, rhythms and dance, body control and gymnastics, and free play. These activities are merely *samples* to illustrate the wide range of available possibilities. You may be primed to devise your own personal variations or extensions of the sample activities as you read and react to the ones presented here.

Although there are no blank spaces on the pages for you to jot down your own inspirations under the headings of *Learning Activities, How Teachers May Use These Activities,* and *How Children May Respond,* we suggest you keep a small notebook with this Series II booklet to correspond with particular suggested activities of *your* ideas, for all the variations *you* may choose to use in teaching, and which *your* children may generate by responding. For instance, if your activity were to generate all the possible "GO" words, the children may have suggestions such as "whoosh," "squirm," or "hustle" to augment the names of locomotor and non-locomotor patterns which we have included in the original activity samples. *Your* ideas and those of your children are just as valid and valuable as ours.

A Word About "Special Needs" Children in Your Classes.
Teachers of young children must always remember that they are interacting with *individuals* rather than a group or class, and that every child has a unique set of needs and interests, strengths, fears, patterns of success and failure, and self-image. It is therefore crucial to plan lessons providing a real range of challenges for children (from easy to difficult). This may be accomplished by including several different activities, or using varied apparatus within the same activity, or sending out more than a single verbal challenge, or in many other ways.

For the "special needs" child (as defined under U.S. Public Law 94-142), it is of particular importance that teachers offer many graduations of activities to balance their lesson planning successfully on the tightrope to adequately challenge each child to his limits and yet remain with the child's capabilities for achieving strong success patterns while conquering worthwhile challenges. Children with mental, social-emotional, or physical disabilities or handicaps can experience success or failure, can build an "I CAN" self-image or an "I CAN'T" outlook just as readily as children who exhibit no such obvious anomalies. Teachers can make a big difference in a "special needs" child's reactions to his world. Sensitivity to student diversities in lesson planning is an excellent place to start building a positive social-emotional and successful climate for all children, no matter what their unique pattern of needs.

What follows here is a partial set of general suggestions for varying the challenges presented to *all* children in attempting to meet their respective needs:

1. ENVIRONMENTAL VARIATIONS
   a. EQUIPMENT
      1. different sizes of balls, bats, or racquets available
      2. different things set out on different days
      3. different arrangements of the same equipment for different sessions
      4. several heights or steepnesses of inclines rather than only one
      5. several pieces to hang from, climb on, jump from
   b. LOCATION — change frequently from gym to playground to room
2. EXPECTATION VARIATIONS
   a. in number of repetitions of a task
   b. in form of the movement response (more or less refined)

c. in duration or intensity of activity
d. in number of responses to a challenge
3. INTERACTION VARIATIONS
    a. simple task requirements to more complex
    b. simple closed statements ranging to open-ended questions
    c. praise contingent on different responses (trying hard, being successful the first time, being successful 4X in a row)

conclusion

We would like to stress the point that the concepts presented here are merely some of the pieces of a puzzle which must be put together by teachers and their children. We realize that all possible concepts relevant to the 2½-8 year-old age group could not be included and that another writing team may have selected entirely different concepts. The concepts and related activities contained in this Series II booklet are only a small sample of the existing possibilities.

To be able to play the game, dance the dance, or perform the gymnastic routine with enjoyment, effectiveness, efficiency, and expression is the major purpose of learning to move. Discovering how one moves and enjoys movement during the younger years is an end in itself, and these are the years of our most concern. To be successful in tennis, equitation, swimming, karate, gymnastics, or dance is of major concern at later ages. The importance of laying the foundation for these later successes is not to be underestimated, and it happens during the early years. The MASTER TEACHER is the one who discovers ways to help each individual young child find enjoyment, satisfaction, and fulfillment in the successful performance of the activities of his choice.

foreword

Physical educators are more and more concerned with the effective development of motor skills, especially in young children when the motor patterns of sport, dance, and gymnastics are established. A body of useful information is now available from the discipline of physical education. The authors of the Basic Stuff series believe that this knowledge can and should be drawn upon by the consumer public to aid teachers in encouraging the growing awareness of children and adults concerning the importance of motor skills in everyday life. The proliferation of activities to which young children may be exposed and the time constraints imposed by school curricula prod the search for and identification of basic concepts that underlie these activities so that the most effective program of movement activities may be presented.

The identification of concepts as an organizing center for school programs of movement activities is not new to education. It is the physical education educators who are slow to recognize the applicability of this approach to our profession. Following World War II, some of the physical education teachers of Great Britain, bored with teaching the same activities to a succession of children year after year, pioneered in their curriculum the adaptation of movement ideas based on the research of Czechoslovakian-born Rudolf Laban. Two of the significant outcomes imported to the United States at the elementary physical education level were Educational Dance and Educational Gymnastics, both which employ a conceptual approach and focus on the development of the individual student *as an individual*. This Basic Stuff series booklet attempts to go beyond this approach to incorporate concepts from other disciplines related to the profession of physical education as practiced by teachers in public schools.

Such an approach represents a major change in teaching strategy. Instead of teaching a series of lessons which include seemingly unrelated activities (such as the games of Four Square, Captain Ball, Beat ball, or a lead-up to badminton), a way can be found to identify concepts which, indeed, relate these separate games in addition to dance, gymnastics, and aquatics in a way which involves positive transfer from one to another. Concomitant knowledge taught in direct congruence to movement activities per se (such as cardiovascular endurance) can be related as well. Another facet of this is that many of these related concepts have direct application in the classroom. For example, when studying the cardiovascular system, students can learn to take their pulse at rest, and then go to the gym for strenuous activity, after which they recheck their pulse to note any differences. While the major strength of this curricular strategy is the involvement of pupils in the thinking process, this fact presented one of the major frustrations for this team: young children *do not think in concepts.* This ability develops over the age span of 2½-8 years, to the point where the utilization of concepts during the latter years becomes realistic. The younger children *do* and then *think;* they then begin to think *as* they act; finally they can precede their action with thought. Our knowledge of child development, and specifically of motor development, dictates that teachers can no longer expect all children to perform the same skill in the same way at the same time. It is educationally more significant that children can either exemplify a concept or skill by *showing* or *explaining.* This poses two problems, particularly for novice teachers who may not have the experience in thinking through enough answers, or may not recognize a new appropriate response when it appears. Teachers have to learn to think as divergently as children. So all the ramifications and outcomes of the processes and products of thinking and moving are *never,* even to the experienced teachers, *totally clear.*

We who have been working with young children know that they are far more capable than we have yet realized. The challenge is now to develop more capable teachers of young children.

Maida L. Riggs

health

Why Sweat It?

Because I Want To Feel Good!

"Health is a state of complete physical, mental and social well being and not merely the absence of disease or infirmity."

World Health Organization

Fitness

What does it mean to me to be fit? I don't get tired and I have more physical power

Learning Experiences: discovering how the heart and lungs work.

Games & Sport
Locomotor patterns
With or without equipment
Over prolonged periods
racing against self/others
circuit training
chasing-fleeing games
dodging hula hoops
jumping rope

1

Rhythms & Dance
Moving to fast music
Singing games: Looby Loo
Dramatizing being strong, fast, fit, well, or healthy

Body Control & Gymnastics
Suspension and support activities
Moving on and off apparatus to music and freezing when
the music stops
Run, jump, roll, and repeat
or
Hang, swing, drop, roll, spring, and repeat

NOTE: The setup of the gym, the choice of music, and the length of time that children are encouraged to perform can be extremely important to this concept. For the purpose of this text, the writing team has chosen the following definition: "Fitness is that state of health which provides children with enough energy to participate in the rigors of a school day without becoming unduly tired."

Focus: the vigor of activity.

How Teachers May Use These Activities

Encourage children to move until out of breath, sweaty, hot, or thirsty.
Request that children count their breaths.
Ask children to take their pulse.
Discuss why hot, tired, thirsty.
Bring in pictures of lean, fit children.
Draw circulatory and respiratory systems.

How Children May Respond

Run until tired; then collapse.
Count another child's breathing/minute.
Watch pulse of another child.
Say: "Being fit means I don't get tired."
Bring picture of fit child and *tell* why it was selected.

Benefits of participation

Why do I participate in physical activity? What are the health benefits?

Learning Experiences: becoming skillful and feeling good.

Games & Sport
Locomotor patterns
    With changes of speed and endurance
    Running with short and long strides
        tagging
        hiding
        dodging
        fleeing
    Non-locomotor patterns with greater range in dynamics
        tighter curls
        stronger twists
        greater stretches
    Manipulative activities with increased accuracy and force
        target for ball
        playground, football
        korfball
        bowling at pins

Rhythms & Dance
Axial patterns with changes of tempo, quality, and emotions
    Expressive patterns
        feeling good
        doing well

Body Control & Gymnastics
    Climbing quickly
    Balancing for a long time
    Hanging and swinging from different body parts
    Sliding fast
    Stretching and twisting
    Bending and turning
    Spinning on scooter or rope

Focus: feeling good about moving.

How Teachers May Use These Activities

Explain the difference in locomotor patterns.
Select children moving with different locomotor patterns.
Have children experiment with different axial movements, or
    with different emotions.

Set out equipment for balancing, climbing, sliding, hanging, and swinging.

Allow time for children to enjoy what they have learned, to use the skill in non-structured free play.

How Children May Respond

Show skill: walk, hop, skip, stretch, and bend.

Explain: "Because I want to play games, run fast, learn to dance, be a gymnast, be healthy."

Say: "Because I want to be skillful and feel good."

Individual differences of physical activity and health

Why does physical activity make *me* feel healthy?

Learning Experiences: expressive body actions.

Games & Sport

Rhythms & Dance

Body Control & Gymnastics

These actions consist of the basic bodily ones which can be built into movement sentences or sequences and pervade the three categories of movement. The children can add to this vocabulary:

Shaking	Collapsing
Swooping	Bouncing
Spinning	Creeping
Pattering	Stamping
Freezing	Quivering
Swirling	Twirling

The activities may be performed with a ball, to rhythm, or on large apparatus.

Focus: how freely children express emotion.

How Teachers May Use These Activities

Suggest a specific word: swirling.

Observe an action performed and select it to be demonstrated to others.

Ask children to suggest a word which shows how they feel.

How Children Respond

Show joy in moving.

Show enthusiasm and zest for trying new things.

Speak their minds.

Participate to the fullest extent.

Show mature emotions.

Being master of actions; not having to live up to the expectations of others.

Feeling good results from a positive self-concept

What can my body do?

Learning Experiences: knowing what the body can do.

Games & Sport

Rhythms & Dance

Body Control & Gymnastics
The body will perform many actions quite naturally. These actions take place on the feet, hands, or other body parts, such as shoulders and hips, and form the basic traveling activities upon which the activities of games/sport, rhythms/dance, body control, and gymnastics are built:

Walking	Jumping
Hopping	Galloping
Running	Rolling
Skipping	Crawling
Stamping	Sliding
Creeping	

Focus: what the child can do.

How Teachers May Use These Activities

Encourage trying a variety of locomotor patterns.
Praise performance (especially on the hop, skip, and gallop).
Discuss a challenging combination of movement patterns.
Observe which foot leads in the gallop.
Suggest hopping on either foot.

How Children May Respond

Repeat activity.
Make decisions about own performance: changing direction on the hop.
Explain which activities are challenging to them.
Persist in problem solving: hop over a line several times.
Respond with enthusiasm to running and turning.

Awareness of the body

What do I feel like
when I move?

Learning Experiences: finding out how the body moves, and what senses contribute to its movement.

Games & Sport
Locomotor patterns with variations
  speeding
  stamping
  hustling
  shuffling
  creeping
  bouncing
  wiggling
Non-locomotor patterns with variations
  twisting
  turning
  stretching
Body parts waking up
Body parts stressed in
  controlling equipment
  leg in kicking
  fingers in releasing

Rhythms & Dance
Recognition and isolation of body parts
Qualities of movement
  sticky, velvety
  gooey, smooth
  shaking, bumpy
  vibrating, prickly
  slow, fast
  hard, soft
Emotions for moving
  happy-sad-joyful
  love-hate-aggression
  shrinking
  horror-hiding
  withdrawal
  protecting oneself
  The Rag doll
  "If You're Happy and You Know It, Clap Your Hands"
  "This Is What I Can Do"
  "Put Your Finger in the Air"
  Aiken Drum

Body Control & Gymnastics
Awareness of body balance and shape with eyes shut
Relationship of body parts
  opposition-together
Body actions
  stillness
  acceleration
  deceleration
  roll over different surfaces
Experiencing tension
Body awareness through touch
  rubbing
  pressing
  holding
  exploring with eyes open and shut

Focus: details of body movement.

How Teachers May Use These Activities

Name body part: "What is it called?"
Explain action of body part: "How does it move?"
Suggest all parts that bend.
Question: "What does it feel like to be upside down?"
Request: "Show me how you move when you are happy."
Name the kinesthetic sense and *ask* children to shut their eyes
  and feel a specific moving part.
Name senses: sight, sound, touch.

How Children May Respond

Show body part.
Name body part.
Find joint that bends.
Explain: "Bending makes it smaller."
Describe feeling in total body or body part: "I feel dizzy."
Experiment swaying when standing with eyes shut.

The joy of experiencing movement

Why do I like to run? **Learning Experiences:** finding out how to create movement showing elevation, vertigo, weightlessness.

Games & Sport
Mimetics of favorite sport
running a broken field
dribbling a soccer ball
throwing a ball
riding a horse

Rhythms & Dance
Dance mime
fun at the circus
going to a fair
a snowball fight
responding to happy music
making a dance

Body Control & Gymnastics
Jumping variations
Skipping variations (with ropes, hoops)
Twirling actions
Running & chasing
Creating a movement sequence
Spinning on a scooter or rope
Sliding and falling

Focus: happy faces.

How Teachers May Use These Activities

Suggest children depict their favorite sport/activity.
Ask children to choose a subject for dance mime.
Set out equipment to evoke jumping with elevation.
State a task which involves a movement sequence: show two (3-4-5) different locomotor patterns, at least one of which shows a twist.
Provide apparatus and surfaces for sliding and falling.

How Children May Respond

Guess what the activity is.
Tell how they knew what sport it was.
Select (individually or in groups) a movement idea and *present* it.
Tell what types of movements (strong, weak, sustained, percussive) give the most pleasure and *explain* why.

Physical activities can help everyone feel good

Why do I feel alive
when I run?

Learning Experiences: learning about body zones

Games & Sport

Rhythms & Dance

Body Control & Gymnastics
The body is naturally divided into several skeletal zones. A significant aspect of feeling good is tied up in being able to use areas of the body in different zones.
Right side
Left side
Front
Back
Upper half of the body
Lower half of the body
Body balance, coordinated movements, and an awareness of space are dependent upon being able to locate and move the body parts in these various zones.
Rocking on front, back, and sides
Rolling in different directions and in different body shapes
Rocking on the hips, back in different body shapes

Focus: feeling good in general.

How Teachers May Use These Activities

Suggest hopping, skipping, sliding to the right.
Suggest galloping, leaping with the left foot leading.
State a task: Make a movement sequence which shows a roll, a rock, and a roll.
Differentiate between a rock and a roll.

How Children May Respond

Show rocking on different parts of the back.
Show rocking on the hips in a curled shape.
Show a right shoulder roll.
Show the difference between a stretched and a curled roll.

11

appearance

Why Sweat It?

Because I Want to Look Good!

Participant's body "looks good"

What makes me look good? (anyone)

Learning Experiences: focusing on efficient, effective movement.

Games & Sport
Agility: run, figure 8s
Total body assembly
jumping
hitting
catching
kicking
throwing
Hand-eye efficiency
catching
hitting, bouncing
rhythm and force in jumping, hitting, bouncing

Rhythms & Dance
Synchrony and rhythm in locomotion

walk	slide
run	gallop
hop	leap
skip	jump

Heads, shoulders, knees, and toes
Combine locomotor and non-locomotor in a rhythmic sequence
jump, twist
jump, bend

Body Control & Gymnastics
Total body assembly
rolling, rocking, stopping, jumping
Symmetry and opposition in climbing and running
Curling, stretching with tension
Resiliency when landing from flight
Symmetry of arms in jumping

Focus: details of movement, especially flow.

How Teachers May Use These Activities

Set up apparatus/equipment which demands total body assembly.
Provide even-uneven rhythmic patterns for locomotion.
Question why one throw results in hitting a target and another does not.
Explain opposition and alternation.

How Children May Respond

Show a light/heavy foot pattern.
Run and *jump* lightly and quickly.
Select a movement that looks best and tell *why*.
Tell why one move is better than another.
Perform a rhythmic/non-rhythmic hop, skip, slide, gallop.

Training for lean body mass

How often and how long should I exercise?

Learning Experiences: focusing on duration and variety of activities for whole body.

Games & Sport
Warm up of continuous . . .
    running, 30 seconds-1 minute
    tagging, chasing
    fleeing
    obstacle courses

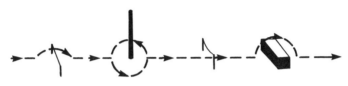

over hurdle   around pole   under rope   on & off box

    jumping jacks
    windmills
  arm, hand, leg, trunk circling

Rhythms & Dance
Vigorous dances
    "This is The Way the Lady Rides"; "Go Round the Mountain"
Stimulating music
  Marches
  "Toreadors"
  "The Love of Three Oranges"
  Sousa marches
  Latin rhythms
  "Reggae"

Body Control & Gymnastics
Combining movements
  on apparatus
  on-off
  over-under
  under-around
  etc.
On floor and repeat on apparatus with a partner
  follow the leader
  cannon/round
  mirroring

Focus: strenuous activity.

How Teachers May Use These Activities

Include strenuous, large muscle activity on a regular basis: at least 20 minutes/day; 300 calories of activity cost.

Pay attention to activities which involve the entire body, especially the upper trunk.

Balance activities to include running, jumping, balancing, hanging, climbing, rolling, sliding, throwing, kicking, bouncing, striking, catching.

Tell why activity helps keep the body thin.

How Children May Respond

Move continuously without bumping or stopping.

Explain why it might be easier to move if thin or short or tall or heavy . . .

Use examples of thin athletes, dancers.

Dynamic form

What makes my skill look strong?

Learning Experiences: focusing on force and flow

Games & Sport
Obstacle courses
Hurdles: two cones and wand
Use of force and speed in throwing, kicking, hitting
Moving and stopping: kicking, dribbling
Imparting energy: throwing and checking movement

Rhythms & Dance
Ethnic and cultural differences in dynamic form: "Muffin Man," "Carousel"
Accents, timing
Repetition: "Row, Row, Row Your Boat"
Phrasing: contrasting locomotor patterns
Music with strong beat; canon form
"Bunny Hop"
"Gallant Ship"

Body Control & Gymnastics
Movement sequence showing changes in speed, force, and flow; levels and directions
Tension and release contrast on apparatus
Rocking and rolling
Yielding to gravity and overcoming it (resisting)
Rebounding on inner tube, Jumping Jimmy, Hippity Hop ball
Balancing on "bongo" board, wobbling balance beam
Symmetrical and asymmetrical balancing

Focus: combination of force and flow

How Teachers May Use These Activities

Present specific dance skills which demonstrate dynamic form: skip, gallop.

Encourage (with music or drum) a sense of timing and phrasing.

Set task: form a continuous marching movement in canon style using swinging ropes.

Make a specific request for children/a child to set up an obstacle course.

Present the problem of setting up an obstacle course: what should it include?

Elicit spontaneous responses to show how to strengthen arms, show force, or flow.

How Children May Respond

Experiment with jumping and rolling.

Explain what makes the body move smoothly.

Beat or clap out rhythmic phrases on floor in movement pattern.

Create dances.

Body as subject

Learning Experiences: reviewing fundamental movements and sensations.

Games & Sport
Locomotor patterns
  walking
  jumping
  hopping
  skipping
  crawling
  sliding
  rolling
Handling objects
  Propulsive
    throwing
    hitting
    kicking
    blocking
  Receptive
    catching
    controlling with stick, racket, scoop

Rhythms & Dance
Emotions
Force-weakness
Response to pulse, rhythm, phrasing
Shapes, designs, floor patterns
Weight-weightlessness
Vertigo
Speed
Balance
Communication
Sensations: hot/cold
Being a pilot, skier, ballet dancer

Body Control & Gymnastics
Balance patterns

standing	twisting
sitting	rotating
bending	swinging
straightening	climbing
stretching	

Supporting another person

20

Focus: variety and quality of movement.

How Teachers May Use These Activities

Review how one moves and how it feels to move.

Ask "What parts of your body do you use to change directions? "How does it feel to be crooked?"

Pose problems which involve using the arms/knees/ankles/hips in jumping.

Point out the function of the eyes in balance: "Jump and turn with eyes closed, what happens?"

How Children May Respond

Imitate the gestures of another child as in the game "Find the leader."

Investigate parts of the body to balance on.

Experiment with ways of supporting another person.

Body as object

Learning Experiences: being manipulated; being active; being the audience; moving to imagery.

Games & Sport
Being a target: Dodgeball
Swinging games: Statues
Partner games: Wheelbarrow
Moving like: snake, wind, clown, skeleton, cloud, snowball, leaf
Falling

Rhythms & Dance
Being a model, an audience
Dances of imitation
"Thread Follows the Needle"
"Five Little Chickadees"
"How Do You Do, My Partner"
"Gallant Ship"

Body Control & Gymnastics
Partner work which involves
pushing
pulling
lifting
supporting
twisting
spinning
dragging
swinging
rolling
sliding
making a bridge

Focus: how children use each other as objects.

How Teachers May Use These Activities

Device examples: roll like a ball, pencil, corkscrew.
Present ethnic dances which include being swung: "Little Brown Jug."
Formulate tasks for partners: Make a movement sequence which involves one support and two other ways of moving your partner (as in twisting or pushing).

How Children May Respond

Stretch like a rubber band then collapse.

Demonstrate how a kite flies.

Make movement sequence: one partner spins the other, both run, jump, roll, and balance with a partner.

Explain the difference between body as passive object and active subject.

Tell what an observer looks for.

Guess what a statue looks like.

Individual differences in performance

Learning Experiences: focusing on developmental, structural, sex, and stylistic differences.

Games & Sport
Movement games of other cultures
  Ambos Ados (Puerto Rico)
Rolling/kicking/chasing ball
Combine: rolling/throwing ball over apparatus
Chasing/evading

Rhythms & Dance
Dances of other cultures with music
Music with contrast
  slow/bouncy
  fast/sustained
Voice sounds
Body noises
  click teeth
  smack lips
  stomp feet
  clap hands

Body Control & Gymnastics
Bouncing on Hippity-hop ball
Alternate running-collapsing/falling
Running, jumping, rolling
Climbing on trestle tree, beam, box, stool
Swinging from rope, bar
Swinging, dropping, rolling sequence

Focus: individual styles of moving.

How Teachers May Use These Activities

Observe energy levels, challenges and preferences.
Select skills to practice, performance to *reinforce*.
Note type and frequency of play.
Set up for wide variety of challenging apparatus/equipment.
Suggest throwing over trestle tree, under stool.
Provide opportunity for quiet and strenuous activity.

How Children May Respond

Show what makes each person feel good.
Tell why each person moves in certain ways.

Set up apparatus/*choose* equipment to show preferences.
Use equipment in a unique way.
Rearrange equipment to create greater challenge.
Talk about experience or accomplishment.
Demonstrate a particular skill.

achievement

Why Sweat It?

Because I Want To Do Better!

Locomotor Movements

What ways are there for me to travel from place to place?

Learning Experiences: varying skills, crawling, creeping, sliding, walking, running, jumping, hopping, rolling, and climbing.

Games & Sport

Giant Steps with cartwheels, rolls, umbrella step, and worm-like motions

Find as many ways to get into, out of, and around a hoop as possible

Find as many ways to get over a stretched rope as you can

Follow the leader: when leader (teacher or child) changes a movement, so must the other children

Experiment with different arm positions when running

Run on toes, with straight legs, prancing, lifting legs high in back

27

Walk changing directions on each fourth beat, each three, two, one

Skip forward, backward, and in a circle

Hop over a ball; around it. Find other ways to get over it

Slide between two lines, first to right and then left

Rhythms & Dance

Be a horse pulling a heavy load; a circus horse, a polo pony

Mimic the toys in Santa's workshop

Move to the music of "Peter and the Wolf"

Body Control & Gymnastics

One partner lies on the floor; the other finds different ways of going over and around: bunny jump, cartwheel, hand spring

Jump from box showing curled, stretched (ball and window), symmetrical, asymmetrical shapes

Roll from one corner of the mat to the other three and back to start without repeating the same kind of roll

Jump over a mat and roll back

Run around gymnasium (playground), jumping over everything you can

Climb up the back side of a ladder and down its front side

Coffee grinder

Focus: use of actions using total body.

How Teachers May Use These Activities

Select different children to be leaders in games or movement sequences.

Choose locomotors to combine into sequences: walk, hop, slide.

Watch for and *reinforce* unique uses of locomotors (step hop, grapevine).

Ask about differences and similarities of locomotor patterns ("How is your skip different from your slide?").

Provide opportunities for different locomotor patterns to even rhythms: walk; hop; run; jump.

Elicit responses for locomotor patterns to uneven rhythmic patterns: gallop; skip; slide.

How Children May Respond

Try own different ways of performing locomotor patterns.

Lead or *follow* other children when using locomotor patterns.

Point out children who are performing locomotors correctly or well ("Carlotta, Maria, and Johann have good leaps — they get really high off the floor").

Describe imagery connected with locomotors before demonstrating those locomotors.

Non-locomotor movements

What movements can I use when I do not move from place to place, or in combination with traveling?

Learning Experiences: pushing, pulling, swaying, stooping, stretching, bending, twisting.

Games & Sport

Swaying from standing, kneeling, and sitting positions

From squat position, twist to tall standing position

Place bean bag on head while in back lying position; come to stand without dropping bean bag

Lifting partner

One partner in back lying position of floor, with body stiff

Partner places hands under ankles and lifts legs off floor

Or, places hands under shoulders and lifts upper trunk off floor

Partners stand back to back gripping each other's wrists over their heads. One partner rocks forward lifting the other on his back. Partners must be of equal height to perform this

Lifting a medicine ball from the floor to an overhead position

Rhythms & Dance

Make yourself as tall as a tree

wide as a house

thin as a pin

small as a mouse

Make a movement grow

begin with the smallest part of your body that will bend and gradually include the whole body. Repeat as drum beat becomes stronger, louder or faster

Music can be chosen which helps the children spin, twist, shake, vibrate, thus bringing in all axial movements

Body Control & Gymnastics

Move your head (hand, shoulder, leg, arm) in as many ways as you can think of. Can you combine all of these head movements, bending sideways, forward, and backward into one movement?

Draw a circular (square, triangular) pattern in the space you are sitting with one part of your body. Make it as large (small) as possible

Touch your fingers to your toes, your knees, your shoulders. Now take your fingers as far from each of these body parts as possible

Find three parts of your body you can twist

Find two parts of your body on which you can turn or spin
Find a piece of apparatus on which you can show a twist and a turn

Focus: use of all body parts in axial movements.

How Teachers May Use These Activities

Direct children to perform combinations of 2, then 3, then 4 or more axials.

Select and *position* apparatus to elicit axial patterns.

Question children about their axial movements ("Which one did you just do with your arms?").

Choose rhythm pattern or music for children to respond to using axial movements.

How Children May Respond

Tell what makes a bend different from a twist, different from a stretch.

Explain correct or incorrect parts of own performance of axials.

Design and perform own unique combinations of axial movements.

Demonstrate and *label* particular axial movements when asked.

Manipulative movements (prehension and dexterity)

How can I control a ball?

Learning Experiences: reaching, grasping, and releasing.

Games & Sport

From sitting, kneeling, standing position, bounce ball around body, clockwise, counterclockwise (to the right or left)

In standing position bounce ball in figure eight pattern around and between legs

Stoop beside ball (or lie down beside it) and begin to pat it As it begins to bounce, begin to jump and make your jumps higher and higher

Toss to self while running, skipping, hopping around the room

Toss to wall and catch while running around the room

Toss over a rope and catch on the other side

Make figure eights among objects or people

Toss over   Bounce around

Body Control & Gymnastics

Ball gymnastics

bounce ball to rhythm with right/left hand/alternate hands

bounce under right, then left leg

toss, catch; toss, bounce, catch; toss, turn, catch

figure eight with one hand/changing hands

Partner work

each partner has ball; toss and catch each other's ball; bounce to each other

make ball routine with partner

Focus: use of fingers and hands.

How Teachers May Use These Activities

Ask about games, dances, or gymnastics activities where particular manipulative actions are important and useful.

Note the manipulative actions, unique variations, or problems (errors) which children show as they move.

Suggest ways to make the manipulative actions more difficult.

Make checklists of correct form elements or items for the manipulative actions and *rate* each child.

How Children May Respond

Experiment with several possibilities for varying the performance of manipulative actions.

Cooperate with others when performing manipulative actions together (throwing and catching).

Find ways to perform manipulative actions in relation to large apparatus as well as with hand-held objects (throw a ball over the vaulting horse while going under it).

Make a rhythm pattern to go with a chosen manipulative action (bounce a ball to "shave and a haircut—two bits").

Complex skills are comprised of locomotor, non-locomotor manipulative skills, balance and perceptual motor abilities

How do I put it all together?

Learning Experiences: tracking and anticipating movement.

Games & Sport
In sitting position toss ball in air, rise and catch when standing

Repeat from back lying position

Jumping rope and bouncing ball at the same time

Game: "The Moving Wall." Beginning in large space running (or with any locomotor pattern) or dribbling without bumping or losing control of the ball, the space gradually gets smaller

Juggling the ball with different parts of the body

Throwing the sling ball

Dodge ball in threes or in twos with one partner against a wall

Rolling a ball up a hill or inclined plane and catching

Rhythms & Dance
"Glow Worm Mixer"

"Paw Paw Patch"

"Norwegian Mountain March"

"Bleking"

"Chimes of Dunkirk"

Working in threes, create a movement sequence showing locomotor, non-locomotor movement, and a balance

Body Control & Gymnastics
Walk low balance beam and bounce ball; toss ball to self or to partner

Jump rope on a low balance beam

One partner makes a bridge and the other crawls under, then jumps over

Partners pass on a balance beam or ladder

Using jump rope in locomotor patterns: skip, hop, rebounding (both in place and while moving forward) backwards, or sideways

Focus: task completion.

How Teachers May Use These Activities

State tasks that involve combinations of skills: "On the apparatus of your choice, find a way to get on using your hands, make an asymmetrical balance, and get off showing a stretched shape."

Provide opportunities for jumping, rolling, twisting, and spinning: "Combine these four words in a movement sequence, either on apparatus or on a mat."

Accept the child's completion of a task and respond verbally to the sequence used. "You did a very nice handstand, followed by a roll and a scale."

State that the children are to hop on the tap of the tambourine, twist when they hear the kazoo, and run on the drum beat.

How Children May Respond

Invent movement sequences with a ball and a bar or a balance beam.

Offer suggestions for parts of the body on which one may twist.

Combine run and a turn; bend, spin, stretch.

Perform dances in time with the music.

The goal for the skill determines the form of the skill

How does my purpose affect the form of my movement?

Learning Experiences: varying the skill to be appropriate in different contexts.

Games & Sport
Locomotion changes
  run fast for springs
  run slower when jogging for endurance
  run zigzag when fleeing or chasing (tag games)
  jump for height, standing distance, at end of a run (running long jump, going up for a catch)
Throw for accuracy, distance, height, kicks, hits (still or moving targets)
"Call Ball"
"Three Player Keep Away"
Contrast
  20-yard run
  20-yard zigzag
  20-yard hurdles
Contrast: throw for height/distance
Contrast: jump for height/distance
Contrast: throwing/catching

Rhythms & Dance
Locomotion for expression: 3/4 run, 6/8, 4/4
Twist like corkscrew, winding top, screwdriver
Running with others (Troika)
Locomotors and axials to show
  emotions (fear, anger, joy, happiness)
  holidays
  seasons, weather (autumn, summer, storm, snowfall)
  animals (zoo, circus)

Body Control & Gymnastics
Locomotors and axials for control
  initiating body motion (jumping, leaping, climbing)
  receiving body weight (balances on several body parts)
  hands and feet for hanging, climbing, traveling on to apparatus, across and off the apparatus
  matching a partner's movements (mirroring)
  making this rounded shape
  holding balance on one foot while changing body shapes
  climbing up and down quickly, slowly

Focus: effectiveness of movement.

How Teachers May Use These Activities

Change environments and tasks to elicit differences in response patterns.

Set out variety of targets, markers, balls, implements, heights, and distances of apparatus.

Question differences in the function of specific body parts for specific movements: fingers for catching/releasing.

Choose children to model who are performing differently:
    right and left-hander;
    tall/short child;
    footwork of child running for fun and one fleeing tagger/fleer.

How Children May Respond

Demonstrate patterns and skill in more than one context, tagging, being tagged.

Explain how body parts move differently when throwing, running, jumping, for different purposes.

Tell what the goal is for each activity or task ("I'm trying to jump far, to throw hard").

Compare and *contrast* how the body parts move to fulfill different purposes such as how the arms are kept close to the body on a spin and go away from the body to stop, how the arms are used in the hurdle and the long jump.

Factors that affect the learner's ability to selectively attend

What do I look at when I catch a ball, climb a ladder, or hold a balance?

Learning Experiences: attending to important cues: visual, auditory, tactile.

Games & Sport
Visual cues
> Tossing, spinning, and catching to self or partner
>> football
>> basketball
>> volleyball
>
> Partners toss and catch two balls simultaneously
> Partners bounce and catch two balls simultaneously
> Bouncing red, green, yellow, blue balls around, in and out or through colored hoops
> Bounce balls with eyes closed to focus on the sound of bouncing

Rhythms & Dance
Auditory cues
> Walk to the beat of the drum
> Shake to the shaking tambourine
> Crawl to the scratchy sound of the tambourine
> Tiptoe to the triangle
> Run lightly to the top of the block
> Increase stretch with low to high pitch on the guitar
> Decrease stretch with the decreased sound (loud to soft) of the drum
> Hard tap on the tambourine: stop

Body Control & Gymnastics
Tactile cues
> Curling toes and fingers around rung of ladder
> Using palms of hand on the caterpillar or inchworm walk
> Flattening the back against the frame or stall bars in hanging
> Rounding the back in the back rocker
> Rocking on the abdomen
> Rocking on the thighs in a swan
> Spotting: Jump with 1/4, 1/2, and full turn

Focus: selection of equipment which permits discrimination.

How Teachers May Use These Activities

Make specific request: "Children with a red ball bounce it around all the red hoops; children with a blue ball bounce it into a green hoop."

Share knowledge: children choose red, blue, green, yellow in this order.

Ask why they think this is so.

Remind children to track the ball as it comes toward them.

Provide opportunities for children to tap out rhythms and use instruments.

Elicit spontaneous responses to what sounds make you feel like moving in what way.

Extend child's ankle, hand, wrist, back on a stretch.

Let children take their hand in a balance.

Prompt children to spot when they jump around.

How Children May Respond

Speak in their heads: "Jump," "Turn."

Experiment with different colored balls for catching, different size for sound of bouncing.

Listen to sound of bouncing ball.

Set tasks for different color balls and hoops.

Devise ways of using a ball, a hoop, and a cone in a game.

Tell what they feel they cannot see or hear clearly, e.g., some mats are the color of the floor and children trip over them.

Explain why rocking on the back is easier/harder than rocking on the abdomen or thighs.

Weight transference (dynamic balance)

How do I keep my
body balanced
while moving?

Learning Experiences: shifting weight smoothly.

Games & Sport

Bouncing or kicking ball while moving, dodging, stopping,
and starting quickly, different pathways, floor patterns
changing direction suddenly

moving at different speeds, changing speeds at a signal

throwing, catching, hitting, kicking with different force

varying force, distance, speed when running, bouncing a
ball

propelling to a motionless or moving target ("leading" a
receiver)

moving to catch or intercept a throw, a kick, a hit, a pass

Rhythms & Dance

Folk and ethnic dances using combinations of locomotors
(Norwegian Mountain March: running and step-hop)

Changing locomotor patterns when music changes (walk,
run, skip, hop, jump, leap, slide, gallop)

Body Control & Gymnastics

Stepping rolling, rocking, back and forth to travel on floor or
apparatus

Twisting and turning while traveling (floor and apparatus)

Sequences of rolling, rocking, stepping, twisting, turning
with different (balance on) body parts

On, off, across, above, below, to the side, over, under,
through, piece of apparatus

Flight patterns (jumping, leaping, from apparatus)

Making shapes in the air

Carving air pathways through space

Focus: smoothness in motion.

How Teachers May Use These Activities

Watch practices; *give feedback on* smoothness of movement.

Request refinement of initial responses, repetition, and practice until smooth patterns emerge.

Point out apparatus or manipulative objects to encourage
experimentation.

Ask questions focusing on which body parts were contributing to the motion and how.

Help children evaluate the quality of their own movements for
themselves.

How Children May Respond

Working alone, in partners, with small groups of three or four on weight transference.

Experiment repeatedly with sequences of skills that are interesting to them.

Invent their own combinations of movements for sequences.

Change patterns of movement, without refining one before trying another.

Tell what movements go into their sequences, why they put these together.

Weight-bearing (static balance) equilibrium is attained when the center of gravity is over the base of support

How do I hold a still balance?

Learning Experiences: maintaining balance.

Games & Sport
Statues (children mold each other's bodies into teacher- or child-selected shapes which must be held)

Twister game (body parts stretch to touch spots on floor over or under other players' arms and legs)

Combative stunts involving pulling or pushing partner off balance while trying to maintain your own

"Feet off the Floor": child with softball tries to hit anyone who has her/his feet on the floor

curled position, hands on floor: raise both legs and hold as long as possible

from squat position place hands on floor, elbows straight; lift right, then left leg. Replace right, then left

from stand, place hands on floor and raise legs as high as possible

Rhythms & Dance
Folk or ethnic dances demanding still balances (Seven jumps)

Musical chairs (hold still balance of designated kind when music suddenly stops, maintain balance until music begins again)

Creative dances including stillness alternated with motion

Body Control & Gymnastics
Balancing on different body parts
high and low
small and large basis of support
upright and inverted positions

Rocking, rolling, stepping into still balances, rolling out and into another balance

Partner balances (partial weight-bearing of other person)

Moving on apparatus to music, stopping to hold a balance when music stops

Still balances into rolling or stepping as safe ways to recover

Experiment with different foot positions on landing from a jump: together, apart, sideways, one in front

Roll and spring out; come out in stride position or into a balance

Swing and drop to a balance

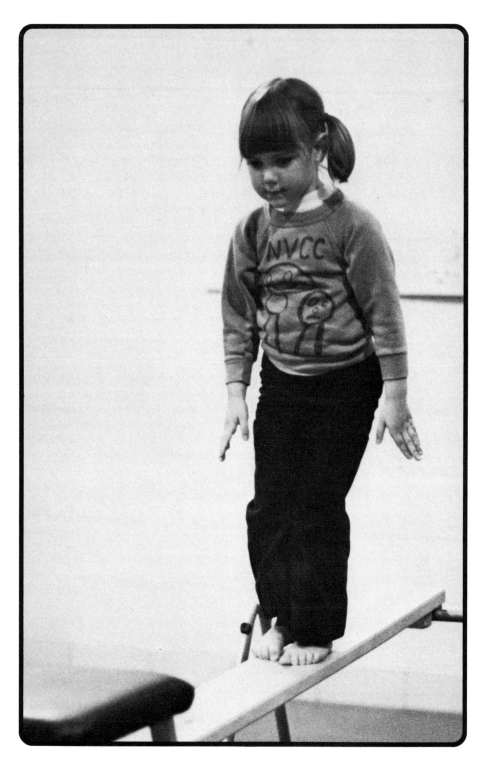

Focus: holding a really still balance

How Teachers May Use These Activities

Label body parts bearing weight during still balance.

Suggest experimenting with narrower or wider base of supports while practicing a movement.

Challenge children to balance wider (base of support), higher.

Ask which body parts are supporting, which are being supported, how to change from one still balance to another one with the least motion in between.

How Children May Respond

Answer questions about supporting body parts, non-supporting ones.

Try changes in base of support, alignment of body parts being supported, to experience near and actual losses of balance.

Invent new balanced positions, alone or with others.

Point to supporting body parts when others are balancing.

Predict in which directions others will lose their balance when they recover from the still balance.

Modify body shape after losing balance from still positions several times.

The body can rotate in 3 planes

How do I move differently in a turn, a cartwheel, and a roll?

Learning Experiences: practicing movement in each plane.

Games & Sport
Running and turning to catch balls
Scooter boards
bending and stretching body parts while spinning and twisting
running and sliding to rotate in different directions

Rhythms & Dance
Ethnic or folk dances with spins and turns
Basic square dance step in teacher-designed sequences (swing partner, do-sa-do, ladies' chain across, swing corner, do-sa-do corner)
Creative dances with turns and spins, with body parts in different relationships (close together, farther apart)
Turns, rolls, and feet-hands-feet patterns to music of varying tempos (very fast, very slow)

Body Control & Gymnastics
Flight off apparatus
jumps and turns
jumps and spins
jumps and flips (somersaults)
changing body shapes during flight
Taking weight on feet-hands-feet patterns (roundoff, cartwheel . . .)
stretching and bending body parts while doing so
Variation in rolling
changing speeds
different directions (forward, backward, diagonal, forward over shoulders, sideward = logroll)
bending, stretching body parts
on floor (mats) to apparatus
Sequences of rolls, turns, feet-hands-feet patterns
teacher- or child-designed
on and off apparatus, across, through . . . on with a turn, off with a roll, over with a stretch, under with a bend . . .
on floor, on apparatus, or combination of floor and apparatus space

Focus: an efficient relation of the body in all three planes.

How Teachers May Use These Activities

Question about use of head, hands, and arms to aid spinning and turning.

Design apparatus setup to elicit rolls, turns, and 2 feet-hands-feet patterns.

Challenge children to roll, turn, or do feet-hands-feet pattern slowly, then quickly — repeat the same patterns.

Call attention to children exhibiting variations in use of body parts to turn or spin more slowly, more rapidly.

Develop movement sequence problems focusing on children discovering relationships between position of body parts and the effect of spinning and turning.

How Children May Respond

Create sequences using a range in the dynamics of motion(slow — fast).

Experiment with different dynamics of the same movements ("spinning faster this way, slower this way").

Analyze another child's movements, labeling them according to the axis of rotation used ("which way is Jason spinning, turning, rolling?").

Force is needed to produce or change motion

How do I make
myself or something
move?

Learning Experiences: moving myself and other objects.

Games & Sport
Manipulative actions
Throwing and catching medicine ball
Ball at rest. Begin hitting it until it begins to bounce
Make it bounce higher and higher
Bounce ball and turn around to catch
Toss higher, bounce, and turn twice to catch ball
Toss and let bounce; repeat letting it bounce twice, then
three, four, and up to ten times. Note changes in height
of toss needed and force applied
Toss ball against the wall and let it bounce once; repeat
and let it bounce two, three, four, and up to ten. Note
angles of toss and amounts of force needed

Rhythms & Dance
Creative dances using contrasting imagery (strong and light
moves)
Features in wind
Heavy piano that doesn't want to be moved
Clouds floating, thunder cloud coming fast
Snowflakes vs. hailstones
Creative dances with jumps and hops imagery (Mexican
jumping beans)
Kangaroos, rabbits, circus tumblers, and trapeze artists
Jump . . .
over a fence
across a stream
to touch a cloud in the sky
over the moon
into and out of a ditch
like a basketball
like a ping-pong ball

Body Control & Gymnastics
Partner work with balancing and taking part of other person's weight
Still balances, moving balances
Traveling while bearing part of partner's weight
Movement sequences involving quick and slow combinations of movements, forceful and soft moves

48

Track and field activites: long jump, high jump, triple jump, shot putting, throwing
Seal slap (slap hands after push off from mat)
Jumping into hoops
L-sit against wall
Jumping over rope

Focus: use of force to create motion.

How Teachers May Use These Activities

Graduate the difficulty level of tasks (shorter to longer implements, targets closer to farther away).

Push for refinement and range of dynamics in the movement responses.

Balance the tasks among games and sports, dance and rhythms, body control and gymnastics.

Question children about forces needed to throw far, jump high, and which body parts produce the motion.

Question how they changed their toss/bounce to let the ball bounce ten times.

How Children May Respond

Assist each other by giving feedback and helping to refine movement sequences.

Work together to create dances or movement sequences.

Name body parts contributing to major action when balancing or manipulating objects.

Explore lots of ways to accomplish the manipulative actions, and persist in trying more and more ways to apply force to own body and objects (propulsion).

The movement path of an object is determined by its speed of rotation and projection velocity

How can I hit a target with a ball?

Learning Experiences: placing a ball where and how you want.

Games & Sport
Ball skills (throwing, striking, kicking)
  against floor
  against net
  against wall
  up a hill
Roll, toss, bounce, throw (overarm, underarm, sidearm)
  over, under objects before bouncing off walls on floor
  with spins from hand twists (to right, left, sideways, topspin, backspin)
  with spins by contacting off center (hit under, above center of ball)
  using hand, foot, paddle, racquet, stick
  varying forces and degrees of spin
  using targets for accuracy
  vary distance, force, direction of propulsion
  back spinning a hoop so it will return
  spinning a ball to go right, left, or return
  toss ball to wall and jump over after first bounce; repeat after second, third, fourth, etc.
  roll a hoop or tire

Body Control & Gymnastics
Jumping from apparatus
  using different forces
  varying length/distance of jump
  varying height of jump protecting body from apparatus to apparatus
  using different body parts to push off
  doing "flips" onto soft crash pad going forward, backward, sideways
  rolls (forward, backward)
Taking off from springboards
  bouncing body into the air
  making different body shapes in the air
  varying angles of take-off

Focus: efficient movement when spinning or projecting objects.

How Teachers May Use These Activities

Emphasize resilience of knees, hips, ankles for soft landings, extension of legs for take-offs.

Set up apparatus at varying heights, distances, from other pieces or from landing areas.

Provide wide variety of sizes and textures of balls, bats, paddles, sticks, racquets.

Give feedback on unique variations from each response.

Probe with questions to lead children to predict effects of spinning the ball or hitting it off center ("where will ball bounce to if you twist it like that? Why does it do that?")

How Children May Respond

Find ways to spin balls to right or left, with top-, back-, or sidespin.

Discover body actions that help child bounce on springboard or as far when jumping for distance.

Help each other by sharing movement patterns that spin balls or make them bounce in particular ways—work on *matching* other child's methods of spinning or bouncing balls

Backspin hoop and jump over it; roll through it.

Specificity of Strength Training

Which muscles do I
want to make
stronger?

Learning Experiences: concentrating on one body part
to become stronger.

Games & Sport
Move the muscles I move . . . three times (each child
becomes a leader)
Pulling, pushing, lifting, boxes
Locomotors up and down inclines or hills
Arm wrestling
Leg wrestling
Combative stunts (pull partner off balance while standing)
Individual stunts ("coffee grinders")
Dual stunts ("Chinese getup" — back to back arms linked,
rise from sitting to standing position)
Toss medicine ball to self
Twister: front bridge to back bridge

Rhythms & Dance
Folk or ethnic dances with jumps and leaps ("Highland
Fling")
Creating dances of strong movement ("work," "mechan-
ical parts," "machines" themes)

Body Control & Gymnastics
Hanging or climbing on ropes
Swinging from arms
Pulling body high levels on apparatus
Pushing body upward from floor
Stretching against resistance
Holding partners while balancing ("Angle Balance")
Curling body parts against resistance

Focus: gaining individual muscle strength.

How Teachers May Use These Activities

Show muscle charts of body.
Name muscles.
Describe locations — simple form.
Sequence tasks so that all muscle groups are used.
Request children to show *strong, heavy* motions.
Select activities which have many repetitions (perhaps allow
for many turns to try . . .).
Choose tasks that gradually require more effort to perform
(can you lift this new box today?).

How Children May Respond

Draw pictures of muscles moving body.

Improve own ways of swinging, hanging, then pushing, pulling . . .

Show different ways to jump, leap in dance context.

Initiate own versions of combative.

Tell which muscles feel tired, which ones need more work.

Devise exercise for a specific muscle group.

Relaxation

How can my body
"let/turn loose?"

Learning Experiences: conscious body relaxation.

Games & Sport

Who can be the tightest spring?

Twist like a corkscrew?

Unwind/unravel like a yarnball?

... other imagery related to showing contrast between
tense/tight, and loose/relaxed muscles

Practice ballistic motion (e.g., throwing kicking, striking
with a long follow-through)

Drop down to floor (at the end of any vigorous game)

Lie down in cotton to breathe deeply, float like a cloud, etc.

Rhythms & Dance

"Flappy and Floppy the Ragdolls"

Dance like a puppet on strings

Be pulled upward to tiptoes and collapse completely to a
puddle or greasespot on the floor

"Wiggle and shake" (vibrate body parts as fast as possible, release tension at sound)

Swing arms and legs to music

Body Control & Gymnastics

Slow, deep breathing, standing high, sitting tall, lying long

Hanging on apparatus from various body parts

Swinging on apparatus with long, loose arcs

Listening to your breathing

Making yourself heavy when lying down

Focus: on signs of tension such as facial expression,
hunched shoulders, fists.

How Teachers May Use These Activities

Call attention to contrasts between tight and loose.

Check relaxation by lifting hands, knees, elbows, feet (flop-
piness).

Observe non-verbal signals of tension when in free play situation or between more formal activities (fingers in mouth,
twisting hair).

Develop muscular tension (tenseness) in activities gradually.

Release muscular tension in activities gradually.

Illustrate tension and relaxation of a muscle, e.g., biceps

Compare and *contrast* feelings from within, from outside ("it feels hard when you touch it," "I feel droopy on the inside").

Find large rubber bands or inner tubes which children may use in a dance.

How Children May Respond

Imitate leader whose muscles get tighter and tighter before releasing tension.

Point to others who are tense/relaxed or to part of body that looks tense.

Invent own imagery for being tense, then relaxed.

Isolate body parts to tense and relax.

Hold body tensely curled when picked up by teachers.

NOTE: What do we mean by "conscious relaxation"? And what does this concept mean to young children? If the muscles of the body are intentionally contracted or stretched, much as a rubber band is stretched, then the opposite, contrasting concept of "letting go" can result in released tension. Relaxation skills are a necessary antidote to some of the child's stress in living in an adult society.

Satisfaction results from attaining goals

Why does reaching my goal make me feel good?

Learning Experiences: trying to reach teacher-selected and self-selected goals.

Games & Sport
Cooperative games: Infinity Volleyball, Earthball
Hitting, throwing, and catching with a partner or small group
Locomotor relays (shuttles, pursuits, circles)
Team games
    net games (manipulative skills)
    running games
    batting games
Propelling, receiving, manipulating on the move (alone, with others)
    controlling self (dodging, cutting, stopping, starting)
    moving with others through space (teammates, opponents)

Rhythms & Dance
Locomotors, axials, manipulative skills in time to music, jumping rope; bouncing, tossing, catching balls; sliding, skipping, hopping, walking, running (+ stylized versions)

Body Control & Gymnastics
Climbing, swinging, hanging, traveling, axial movements
    to match a partner
    to copy a partner
    to lead a partner
    to mirror a partner
    to maintain the shape of a group
    simply for having fun

Focus: having fun and achieving at the same time.

How Teachers May Use These Activities

Discuss with children ways to have fun during activities.

Focus on helping children to understand what they accomplish, achieve, attain, and *do* themselves.

Provide opportunities for doing things together as well as alone, for *talking* about feelings and accomplishments as well as doing the movement patterns.

How Children May Respond

Select favorite ways to move.

Choose most liked balls, implements, apparatus, place to work.

Tell about feelings when experiencing success and failure.

Experiment with changing goals to match performance realistically, and performance to match goals.

Describe how personal goals (or group goals) were achieved and the resulting feelings.

Repeat preferred activities.

Change preferred activity to achieve more success.

Goals need to be realistic

How can I learn to predict how well I can do?

Learning Experiences: improving the match between predictions and performance.

Games & Sport

Partner challenges with axials, locomotors, manipulative skills (both do, then compare with *prediction*, not *person*)

Can you do what you say you can do?

Jump and turn about?

How high can you . . . (leap and land softly)?

How far can you . . . (kick a ball)?

How hard can you throw?

How accurately can you . . . ?

How fast can you . . . ?

Tag games ("I will catch 3 people")

Side or team chase games (Crows and Cranes) ("We'll get 4 more this time")

Rhythms & Dance

Creative dances using imagery (scrambling eggs, frying bacon, popping popcorn, floating balloons)

describe your dance

do your dance

Planning and creating dances to familiar music (each child or small group telling about their performances)

use locomotors

try axials

combine locomotors and axials

Body Control & Gymnastics

Movement sequences using hanging, traveling, swinging, climbing, any combinations (children make these up, alone or in groups; write the movements or say them)

Select heights to climb to, jump from, balance on

Focus: getting closer to your predictions about performance.

How Teachers May Use These Activities

Guide children toward setting and attempting to meet their own goals.

Suggest pattern for predicting performance, trying a task, evaluating achievement, setting new goals.

Ask who can do a cartwheel.

Provide opportunities for children to tell what a goal is and to explain what it means to them to have a goal.

Elicit spontaneous responses: "That was a fine climb up and down the ladder, how could you make it more difficult?"

Present problems such as those used in circuit training and have each child change each problem to fit his goal.

How Children May Respond

Name the specific goals they are trying to achieve.

Predict own performance limits (how high, how far, how much).

Modify group-derived goals to *challenge* own individual capabilities.

Share predictions of goals and actual achievements with others.

Discuss how to make goals realistic for themselves.

Watch others try a task after hearing their predictions and *evaluate* the results (did/did not achieve goal; why/why not?).

Select own equipment or group to work with or movement patterns when given choices.

Personal progress: quantitative, qualitative

How can I improve my movements?

Learning Experiences: becoming *more* accurate, faster, stronger, smoother . . .

Games & Sport
Locomotor races for distance in given time, or given distance for faster times
> around/across room
> around 2 pieces of apparatus

Add own variations when tagger in a game
> holding on to body part, with hands clasped behind back
> teacher tosses ball/hoop into air; children hit or go through it with their soft (sponge) ball
> children walk around space keeping ball/balloon in air with hands, stick, racquet

Target accuracy (still and moving with other people) for throwing, kicking, sending, rebounding ball on different parts of body (with head, knee, shoulder, elbows)

Rhythms & Dance
Make up own dance steps and gestures to familiar music ("Turkey in the Straw")

Repeat basic movement pattern varying gestures, floor pattern, pathway, levels, and body shape to repetitive music (Ravel's "Bolero")

Folk dances with varied rhythms ("Seven Jumps") or increasing tempos ("Hora")

Creating own dance steps, rhythmic pattern to show quality of movement

Body Control & Gymnastics
Hanging, climbing, swinging on apparatus to help develop good body alignment

Upright and inverted balances, changing shapes and/or body parts used for support, moving to/at different levels

Creating weight bearing movement patterns with others traveling onto, on, and off pieces of apparatus

Moving from floor to and from apparatus by stretching and bending

Pushing off apparatus with feet and hands for greater height, distance, and speed to help strengthen the arches of the feet and hands

Focus: quantitative and qualitative changes in movement patterns.

How Teachers May Use These Activities

Set up stations to practice several single skills.

Repeat activities to allow *review* and improvement.

Collect data on children's improvements in several sequenced lessons.

Present problems based on changes in distance, speed, accuracy, endurance, or Laban's four elements of movement.

State individualized, progressive goals for similar tasks.

How Children May Respond

Predict performance improvements (can run 1/10 second faster).

Record evidence of getting better (jumped over rope 10 times).

Share feelings about getting better ("I feel stronger").

Describe areas of specific skills improvement ("I pushed harder with my toes").

Experiment with movement variables subject to change
use of space
how quickly one moves
variations in effort expended
dribbling among other children without bumping or losing control

Comparing with others

Learning Experiences: isolating elements of movement that make people move the same or differently.

Games & Sport
Locomotion comparing with others
accuracy (hopscotch)
distance (races for endurance)
correct form (partner describes)
speed (races) you perform
Non-locomotion/axials with others
vary gestures, body shapes, body parts moving
Manipulation with others
leader-follower games
matching farther, longer, higher, faster, more
target games comparing accuracy
throwing, kicking, sending with other body parts

Rhythms & Dance
Moving in pairs, 3s, 4s, Troika, Schottische for 3
Changing shapes, directions, levels, pathways on accented
beats
Matching the music and a partner's moves

Body Control & Gymnastics
Movements matching other
exact mirroring (frontfacing)
exact matching (side by side)
exact copying (front to back)
exact canon (round) (1st, 2nd)
performed on floor, on apparatus
doing opposite movements (me high, you low)
changing level, speed, direction, body shape
you go first, then I match: climbing, hanging
balancing alone, together

Focus: movement comparisons.

How Teachers May Use These Activities

Question about likeness/difference in children's movement
patterns.
Ask for original movement sequences to be copied.
Point out similarities and differences of sequences.

Challenge to perform exactly like partner, differently from
partner.

Label movement variations seen.

How Children May Respond

Explain how moving the same or differently feels ("it was easy,
hard").

Compare performance with others ("John threw higher, I
threw faster").

Cooperate with others to match, mirror, or copy.

Analyze own unique patterns ("I always like to go fast").

Controlling aggression

Why do I want to hit something?

Learning Experiences: discovering the limits of force.

Games & Sport
Bogey Ball
> teacher rolls ball to other end of gym, children try to beat it
>
> roll hoop and try to run through it, throw ball through, roll through
>
> juggling to keep ball in the air
>
> tapping the ball into air with alternate hands
>
> jumping the shot
>
> batting a ball off a tee
>
> kicking/throwing a ball against the wall
>
> kicking/throwing for distance
>
> double Dutch, double Irish (rope jumping)
>
> Tether Ball

Rhythms & Dance
Creating a dance showing aggression
Showing contrast
> stomping/prancing
> punching/recoiling
> exploding/recovering
> bullying/cowarding

Body Control & Gymnastics
Shadow boxing
Punching a hanging ball, jumping on a crash pad
Racing on scooters
Twisting on a Twisterboard
Balancing on a balance board
Moving with control throughout the apparatus

Focus: channeling aggression into constructive action.

How Teachers May Use These Activities

Use music which contrasts heavy/light, angry/happy.

Set up zigzag course for running, tricycles, or scooters.

Organize group games which demand cooperation.

Provide individual ropes for jumping the rope: child doubles rope and swings it under his own feet.

Discuss possible ways of channeling or controlling aggression.

How Children May Respond

Crush a balloon by stomping on it.
Kick, hit at air.
Mimic a fight they saw.
Pretend being hit.
Discuss being mad, wanting to hit someone.
Hold a group discussion on controlling force.

psycho-social

Why Sweat It?

Because I Want To Get Along!

Self-confidence

What am I able to do
and willing to try?

Learning Experiences: establishing challenges for performance.

Games & Sport
Jumping for height
high jump standard
wand on cones, series = hurdles
Jumping or distance
Throwing for
speed
distance
accuracy

Kicking for
  speed
  accuracy
  distance
Running for distance
  1/4 mile, 1/2, 3/4, 1 on a track
  cross-country, variable distances
  running for speed
  25-yard dash
  hurdles
Running fast among others as still or moving obstacles

Rhythms & Dance
Dance steps
  schottische
  polka
  tour jeté
  buzz

Body Control & Gymnastics
Falling
Rolling in different shapes
  straddle
  curl
  straight
Vaulting in different body shapes
Jumping on/off/over objects in different body shapes
Sliding/hanging on different body parts
Tasks: show your highest balance; a body shape with your
  feet higher than head; a swing, jump and roll; a jump
  with a turn and a roll
Children set out equipment to show self-confidence in
  balancing
  climbing
  jumping
  swinging
  hanging
  falling

Focus: how willingly children try.

How Teachers May Use These Activities

Structure the environment for climbing high, jumping from
  and balancing at the different heights, with differing widths
  and angles of inclination.

Select or *set out* equipment the children have never seen before.
Ask if anyone needs help and *hold out* hand if they do.

How Children May Respond

Take teacher's hand.
Persist at solving a problem.
Perform with astonishing skill and variations.
Put together novel arrangements of apparatus.
Join readily in group games/dances.
Volunteer solutions/answers.

NOTE: It is imperative that the teacher help the child *find* a way on and off apparatus either by saying, "Put your foot here" or by placing the child's foot in a secure place. Children who are lifted on and off apparatus do not become confident, competent decision makers. They must be helped to take responsibility for their decisions and to learn what they can do realistically and safely.

Self-concept

How do I feel about myself?

Learning Experiences: reinforcing skills through practice; daring to try new ones.

Games & Sport
Combinations of locomotor patterns
  walk-hop
  run-leap
  jump-hop
Variations
  walk-hop with turn
  run-leap with change of direction
  jump about — hop forward
Variations in kinds of balls to manipulate a ball
  Korf, whiffle, frisbee
  foot, soccer, playground
Select partner and make up a game with the above equipment

Rhythms & Dance
Show opposites
  boldness-cringing
  fearless-afraid
  success-failure
  familiar-strange
  good-bad
  happy-sad
Create dance
  The Moving Me
Ethnic dances of celebration
  "Oats, Peas, Beans"
Movements of city and country people

Body Control & Gymnastics
Beams of different heights and widths (1', 2', 3', 4', 5')
Task: find ways of balancing on one body part, then move to another on floor; put the sequence on a beam
Task: travel in a variety of ways on feet, hands and feet, hands then feet; put on the trestle tree or ladder
Task: find spaces and equipment that allow traveling by jumping, swinging, hanging, sliding

Focus: facial expressions.

How Teachers May Use These Activities

Develop appropriate vocabulary for expression of feeling about self: strong, buoyant, tired, happy.

Design tasks to demonstrate feelings about self.

Have children draw themselves moving.

Ask children to beat out a rhythm and move to show how they feel about themselves.

Provide range of percussive instruments: bells, triangle, tambourine, sticks, drums with ethnic sounds.

Use simple language appropriate for ethnic group: uno, dos (Spanish; Une, deux (French); Wanche, nopa (American Indian); eins, zwei (German).

How Children May Respond

Show how they feel (good, glad, . . .)

Tell how they feel, and why.

Select music to portray how they feel.

Select apparatus on which they feel competent.

Design tasks showing how they feel.

State: "I am best when . . ."

NOTE: Caution should be exercised in comparing children's actions when it might affect self-concept. One child may jump from a place that is as high as the child is tall while another jumps from heights only half as high, but both can feel good about what they have achieved. A child with a good self-concept is aware of his limits.

Satisfaction and affiliation needs

Do I like to play alone or with someone?

Learning Experiences: adapting activities/partners.

Games & Sport
Solo games
    Jumping rope
    One-Two-Three O'Leary
Partner games
    Back to Back
    Partner Tag
Group games
    (variations in locomotion)
    Squirrel in Trees
    Ring Call Ball
    Pussy Want a Corner
    Run, Rabbit, Run

Rhythms & Dance
Folk/Square dances
    "Seven Steps"
    "Nuts in May"
    "Marusaki"
    "Come Skip with Me"
    Creative dances with partner, group, solo
Dancing to music of choice
Walk
    in snow boots
    in deep mud or snow
    through tall grass
    on hot bricks
    past a sleeping baby
    looking for something you've lost

Body Control & Gymnastics
No apparatus
    climb through arms
    bear, crab, duck walks
    bunny, crow, kangaroo hop
Apparatus
    horizontal ladders: weave through
    spring board: jump and roll
    bar: circle
    vertical ladder: climb back side
    inner tube: rebound side to side

scooter: spin
bench: bunny jump; jump and turn
beam: Angel Stand, scale

Focus: children's selection within activity areas.

How Teachers May Use These Activities

Offer alternative selections from
   games and sport;
   gymnastics and body control;
   rhythms and dance.
Note preferences children exhibit.
Reinforce preferences they show.
Follow-up by questioning "why that choice?"

How Children May Respond

Show preference in selection of equipment, use and duration
   of involvement, choice of partner or group.
Explain reasons for preference of partner/activity/equipment.
Tell what satisfaction means.

NOTE: This is undoubtedly one of the most important concepts for this age group since they tend to repeat that which
gives them satisfaction, if given the choice. A playful atmosphere reinforces the enjoyment children receive and should
pervade the learning situation for this young age group at all
times and in all places.

Cooperation

What is it like to
work/play with
someone else?

Learning Experiences: sublimating personal impulses
for group goals.

Games & Sport
Long rope jumping

children run through front door;
dribble ball through

or

shuttle zig-zag relay;
running, with baton, other locomotors

Rhythms & Dance
"Tinikling"
"Red River Valley"
Flower dance
children move as petals (in single group)
Active and passive partners as in "How Do You Do My
Partner"
Create dance depicting cooperation; contrast cooperation
and group dissonance

Body Control & Gymnastics
Matching movements with balls, jump ropes, scarves,
wands
Partner support: Leap Frog
Two contest with each other: wrestling
Counterbalance one another's weight: partner swing
Help partner jump; Chinese Get Up
Task: all children get from point A to B on apparatus setup
without stepping on the floor.

Focus: how children relate to others.

74

How Teachers May Use These Activities

Plan dual stunts/activities which elicit cooperation.
Lead discussion on cooperation.
Show examples of teamwork in
 sport,
 dance,
 gymnastics,
 play.
Demonstrate ways of lifting, moving, setting up apparatus in
 2s, 3s, or small groups.
Establish safety rules for partner/group work.
Have children discover ways of working together:
 side by side (same/opposite facing);
 follow the leader;
 back to back;
 facing;
 antiphonal/echo;
 canon.
Suggest movement patterns for working together.
Assign responsibilities.

How Children May Respond

Follow directions.
Make up rules which delineate group goals.
Discuss cooperation.
Select music consonant with working together.
Select apparatus/equipment for partner work.
List ways of cooperating:
 obeying, following;
 using ideas/making ideas;
 working together, as in lifting equipment.
Select responsibilities.

Competition

What is it like to
work against
somebody,
enhancing
movement or
maximizing
personal goals?

Learning Experiences: competing with self and with others.

Games & Sport
Group games
Kick Over, Captain Ball
Long Ball, Long Base,
Keep Away in 2's, 3's
Shuttle Relays: lead up to high jump/hurdle
Practice
evading
dodging
gaining possession
Tug of war
Throwing, jumping for distance

Rhythms & Dance
Portray competition as in football dance
Create a dance: "Struggle"
Dance ideas
win
lose
"skunk"
compete

Body Control & Gymnastics
Partner wrestling: arm, leg
Pull off balance
Partner work in opposition
on-off
high-low
fast-slow
straight-crooked
on the floor or apparatus

Focus: ways of *bettering* one's own performance.

How Teachers May Use These Activities

Distinguish between winning and losing, competing with self
and against others.
Have children clearly identified for competition, e.g., pinnies.
Help children set goals for improving their performance.

77

Discuss winning strategies:

    throwing ahead of teammate;

    evasive tactics (feinting, dodging, blocking opponent's
      pathway).

Challenge children to alter, improve, try new apparatus/
    equipment by suggesting specific ways: "Try stretching
    toward my hand on the next cartwheel."

How Children May Respond

Show changes of footwork in fleeing/chasing/overtaking.

Mime hitting, being hit, falling.

Discuss ways of bettering

    speed,

    strength,

    endurance,

    ideas,

    accuracy,

    score,

    cooperation.

Decide ways of

    negotiating,

    officiating,

    arbitrating.

Make up competitive game.

Make rules for new game.

Modify rules.

Discuss strategies for arbitration, negotiation.

Communication

What do I tell
people with my
body?

Learning Experiences: acquiring the skills of non-verbal communication.

Games & Sport
Find the leader using axial and locomotor movements
Follow the leader
  including rolling, twirling, spinning
Sport signals: out, foul, safe, out of bounds, goal

Rhythms & Dance
Pantomime daily events: going to school, playing after
  school, weather changes
Hand and body gestures: come, go, stop, bad, shame
Depict
  straight as . . .
  crooked as . . .
  curled as . . .
  collapsed as . . .
  sleepy as . . .
Respond to another child's rhythm

Body Control & Gymnastics
Modeling the body into shapes like clay
Partner work:
  shapes as theme; A makes a shape, B matches/makes an
    opposite one or the same in a different position
Group work on or off apparatus
  Choose a series of shapes and move between them:
    round to arrow; square to round; symmetrical to
    asymmetrical
Question and answer with body movements

Focus: use of body as instrument of communication.

How Teachers May Use These Activities

Ask for portrayal of how children feel
  when it is thundering,
  when the wind blows,
  when it snows,
  happy to see someone,
  having won/lost a game.
Bring pictures of athletes/dancers/gymnasts and discuss
  movement differences in how they communicate.
List words and gestures used in competition.

79

How Children May Respond

Write/draw, then *move* to a day's activities.

Tell what sport/dance/gymnastic event they saw.

Describe how to distinguish between the movements of a dancer and a soccer player, a . . . and a . . .

aesthetics

Why Sweat It?

Because I Want To Turn On!

Social benefits of physical activity

Why do I like to play with others?

Learning Experiences: discovering the skills of playing with others: taking turns; having partners; relating; using someone else's idea; being an example; sharing ideas.

Games & Sport
Partner games: Partner Tag
Dual games: contesting (Hopscotch, Tether Ball, Handball)
Group games: cooperating
Group games: competing
  Red Light, Four Square
  ''Passing the Stone''
  receiving
  retaining
  seizing
  getting rid of

Rhythms & Dance
Creating dances together
Dance drama: the Seven Dwarfs
Dance composition: Bullfight
Ethnic dances:
  "Tanko Bushi"
  "Hokey Pokey"
  "Greensleeves"
Expressive: "Red Riding Hood and the Wolf"

Body Control & Gymnastics
Matching movements; mirroring
Working *without* contact: meeting, leaving, passing by
Working *with* contact but without sharing body weight
Partner work and/or group work: jumping together on an innertube or tire
Making letter with the body: "Y"; with a partner: "X"
Supporting a hand stand
Rocking together on a Banana
DOUBLE FORWARD SCALE

Focus: how children select and then relate in groups of various sizes.

How Teachers May Use These Activities

Plan partner or group work including possible responsibilities within the group.
Discuss cooperation with each other including partner support.
Show how one child can help another on/off apparatus.
Pose problems which require cooperation.

How Children May Respond

Work together to set up apparatus.
Make up a cooperative game like "Shipwreck".
Tell why they like to compete.
Experiment with different ways of supporting a partner.
Explain with whom they like to play.

Subjective aesthetic

How can I maximize "feeling good?"

Learning Experiences: emphasizing qualitative experiences, the "flow" of movement sequences.

Games & Sport
Moving the body into different zones of space: pathways; patterns; levels
    weaving
    zig-zagging
combining axial and locomotor moves
combining small and large footwork

Rhythms & Dance
Stopping the flow of movement, resulting in different shapes or attitudes of the body
Having the body draw a shape in space
    arrow-like
    round
    twisted
    crooked
    flat

Body Control & Gymnastics
Balancing and over-balancing
    balance → roll → balance
    balance on or off apparatus
    symmetrical and asymmetrical balance → roll → balance

Focus: outward signs of feeling good (facial expressions, body gestures and postures).

How Teachers May Use These Activities

Ask what is meant by "flow" of movement.
Can you move slowly into a twisted shape followed by a round shape?
State: "Make a zig-zag air pattern with a part or the whole of your body."
Say: Find a way to balance on a partner or piece of apparatus, then roll into another balance."

How Children May Respond

Show a run followed by a "frozen" balance on one foot.

Twist slow motion into a corkscrew shape.

Bring in pictures of different shapes in movement.

Perform a handstand—forward roll—scale.

Make a movement sequence from a V-sit into a backward roll and a knee stand.

Objective aesthetic

How can I use my
body to
communicate?

Learning Experiences: finding out how to show *intent* of movement.

Games & Sport
    Propulsion skills
        tossing
        throwing
        punting
        kicking
        rolling
        striking
        bouncing or dribbling
        bump or set
    Receipt skills
        catching
        trapping
    Feinting actions
        movements in space
        small and large steps

Rhythms & Dance
    Action images taken from
        Nature: wind, water
        Noises: hiss, grunt
        Words: pop, burst, fiddle-faddle
        Chants: Humpty-Dumpty
        Animals: lame dog
        Mechanization: wheels
        Outer space: blast off
        Colors: red, black
        Sculpture: statues
        Sports: wind sailing
        Story play: "Robert the Rabbit"
                "The Robin Family"
                "A Smile in the Snow"
                "The House on the Hill"*
                "The Visit"
    Sounds of animals: baa baa
    Things: toot-toot
    Activity: giddy-ap
    Nonsense: higgledy-piggledy

*Peck, pp. 117-147.

Body Control & Gymnastics

Balancing with different body shapes and on different body parts; different objects
flight
opposition: pushing, pulling
body actions: lifting, dropping

Focus: exaggeration and magnitude of movements.

How Teachers May Use These Activities

Ask children to show how they would move if being chased, playing football, having a fight.
Present the choice of moving like an automobile or a plane.
State task of finding different positions of balancing with hands and feet on the floor or on a piece of apparatus.
Read a story/play.

How Children May Respond

Pretend to be afraid of a chasing dog, happy while running.
Discuss (show) how the sounds and movements of auto and plane might differ.
Balance with
  two hands and one foot,
  two feet and one hand,
  one hand and one foot (same/opposite),
  two hands and two feet.
Mime emotions.

coping

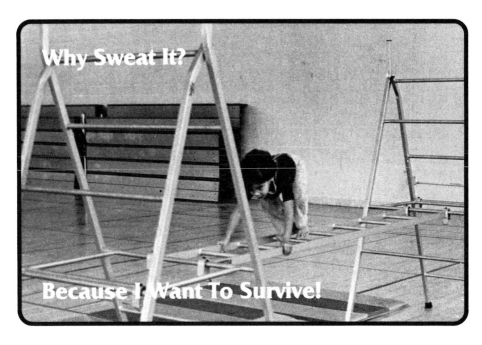

Why Sweat It?

Because I Want To Survive!

Well-conditioned muscles help to maintain good body alignment and help to prevent injuries

How can I keep from getting hurt?

Learning Experiences: learning what can be done safely.

Games & Sport
Rubber bands (stretching all muscles)
Running games to develop endurance (play longer each time)
Jump for distance or height

Rhythms & Dance
Jumping rope (many variations)
Locomotors and axials for longer periods of time in rhythm with sounds or music

Imagery of tallness and straightness
    walk like puppeteer is pulling the string through the top of your head

Body Control & Gymnastics
    Stretching, bending, twisting, on floor and apparatus to develop flexibility
    Balancing on various bases of support (upright and inverted)
    alone or with others
    Helping set up and take down apparatus
    Climbing, swinging, hanging to develop leg and arm and shoulder girdle strength
    Jumping and leaping from varying heights of apparatus and varying distances
    Simple yoga stretches

Focus: increasing strength, flexibility, and endurance.

How Teachers May Use These Activities

Encourage repetition of activities for building strength and endurance in every lesson.

Provide opportunities for stretching all muscles.

Challenge children to compete with themselves to meet their goals for strength, endurance, and flexibility.

Set up equipment and apparatus to elicit stretching, bending, and twisting.

Present movement problems to elicit repetitions of movement skills for strength and endurance.

How Children May Respond

Maintain balances in various positions.

Increase weight of objects lifted, carried, or moved by pushing or pulling.

Are able to climb and swing higher and longer, jump farther, and run longer.

Try to sit and walk "tall" with body parts in good alignment when doing ordinary tasks outside the physical activity lessons.

Surviving in emergencies: developing "an adequate level of physical fitness"

How much fitness do I need to play?

Learning Experiences: to build muscular strength, cardiorespiratory endurance, and flexibility.

Games & Sport
Locomotor, non-locomotor/axial, and manipulative games
    play longer time periods
    take fewer time-outs for rest
    running, leaping, jumping, skipping games
    dodging, starting, stopping games
    throwing and running games
        (based on basketball skills)
    hitting and running games
        (based on racquet sport skills)
    kicking and running games
        (based on soccer skills)
    dribbling a ball while running
    carrying and sending while running
        (maze-type skills for twisting and stretching)

Rhythms & Dance
Folk and ethnic dances using lots of vigorous movement
    (Seven Jumps, New Dance, Polkas)
Created dances using locomotors
    machines, "work" dances
    imitations of animals, sports players
    jumping rope (individual and long rope turned by 2)

Body Control & Gymnastics
Twisting, turning, stretching, and bending to move on, across, off apparatus
Climbing cargo nets, tall ladders (vertical), moving across horizontal ladders to build arm strength
Climbing and traveling on Whittle apparatus for leg and arm strength
Hanging from different body parts on apparatus
Swinging on even/uneven bars
Tug-o-wars (in 2s, 3s, 4s, . . . 2 sides)

Focus: pushing toward one's own capacity in strength, endurance, and flexibility.

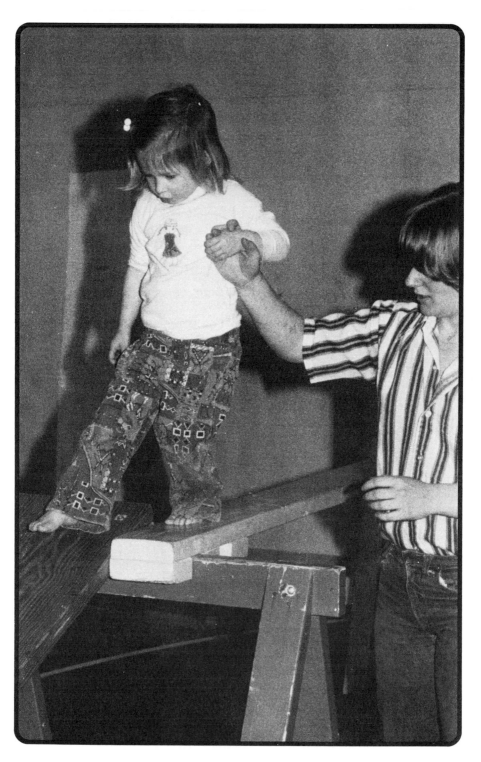

How Teachers May Use These Activities

Promote "doing better than myself" as an ongoing challenge by children for themselves.

Choose games, dances, gymnastics activities with "nonstop" movement.

Build in "ground rules" to enhance probability of very vigorous, continuous movements.

Prompt and *reinforce* discussion of "fitness" concepts mentioned in focus of learning experiences.

How Children May Respond

Volunteer own examples of activities designed for fitness.

Keep record of own progress on teacher- and child-designed tasks over a period of time, and *note* improvements.

Choose preferred activities to do within any single fitness category, e.g., cardiorespiratory endurance.

Explain concepts of fitness and which activities are good for which concepts.

Actively engage in fitness activities.

The meaning of personal movement experiences

Learning Experiences: to build up speed to be safe, strength not to get hurt, agility to get around, and total body assembly to stay on balance while still or moving.

Games & Sport
　Manipulative skills
　　throwing at targets, for distance
　　kicking to others
　　dribbling among obstacles
　Catching when motionless or moving
　Hitting stationary and moving balls (rolling, thrown, bouncing)
　Locomotion: starting, stopping, dodging games (What Time Is It, Mr. Bulldog?, Red light, Green light, variations of tag)
　Chasing and fleeing games (several taggers)

Rhythms & Dance
　Creating dances to act out poetry
　　(emotions, stories, seasons)
　Making dances to imitate colors of the rainbow sequence of a rainstorm, the first winter snowfall
　Making dances to express
　　the spookiness of Halloween
　　the loudness of thunder
　　the brightness of lightning

Body Control & Gymnastics
　Moving on, over, under, around, through, above, across, behind, to the side of apparatus setups
　Moving through teacher- or child-made obstacle courses
　Balancing in upright and inverted positions on the floor and apparatus setups
　Maintaining symmetrical and asymmetrical still and moving balances
　Moving across narrow surfaces using body parts to balance

Focus: building safety awareness and knowledge of personal capabilities.

How Teachers May Use These Activities

Develop large variety of opportunities for tracking, spotting, and focusing on objects.

Prompt children to verbalize descriptions of their movements, reasons why they are practicing the skills, and how they feel when moving or after moving.

Present problems focused on building speed, strength, agility, and balance.

How Children May Respond

Portray being sad, happy, angry, joyful.

Answer questions about feeling while moving.

Share examples of experiences when moving helped cope with environmental emergencies or situations.

Draw pictures representing speed, strength, agility, and balance as ways to cope.

Investigate own and others' speed, strength, agility, and balance while moving.

Andrews, G. ed. *Children's Dance*. Washington, DC: American Alliance for Health, Physical Education, and Recreation, 1973. [Excellent source for ideas, especially examples in imaginary sources for movement and equipment.]

Boorman, J. *Creative Dance in the First Three Grades*. New York: David McKay Company, 1969. [An excellent source for guided experiences in ways the body moves, use of time, energy, space in action, and ways in which it is possible to work with others in dance; material of a lesson is set out, task stated clearly, and time allowed for discovery and performance.]

Briggs, M. M. *Movement Education*. Boston: Plays, Inc., 1975. [The purpose of the book is to provide concise guidance in presentation, development, and progression of movement for children; provides examples of how to meet children's needs and to guide them in developing and perfecting their own movements; special emphasis is placed on encouraging children to arrange apparatus and work out movement sequences.]

Buckland, D. *Gymnastics. Activity in the Primary School*. London: Heinemann Educational Books Ltd., 1969. [The child is asked to explore ways in which the body can move; is required to think about the way in which weight moves from one point of support to another, the speeds employed, the directions taken, and the effort used; the focus is on the child, on decision-making, on selecting and considering the quality of movement; the creative teaching of gymnastics ensures success.]

Burton, E. *The New Physical Education for Elementary School Children*. Boston: Houghton Mifflin, 1977. [A good source for information about spatial awareness, kinesthetic awareness, body awareness, basic movement skills (locomotors and non-locomotors), manipulative skills, and basic sports skills, with short chapters on games, gymnastics, and dance; lesson suggestions organized around a central concept with activities fitting that concept.]

Castle, S. *Face Talk, Hand Talk, Body Talk*. New York: Doubleday, no date. [This book contains photographs of children communicating a range of emotions by using their faces, hands, and bodies.]

Dauer, V.; and Pangrazi, R. *Dynamic Physical Education for Elementary School Children*. Minneapolis: Burgess, 1979. [A classic activities-oriented "traditional" elementary physical education sourcebook with suggested activities covering everything from fitness to track and field for young children.]

Dimondstein, G. *Children Dance in the Classroom*. New York: Macmillan, 1971. [A dance book which emphasizes teachers preparing for dance lessons by understanding basic Laban terminology about movement actions and concepts, by creating a positive and supportive atmosphere for children, and by relying heavily on the use of imagery as a basis for children creating their own dances (no structured folk, ethnic, or square dances included).]

Elliot, M.; Anderson, M.; and LaBerge, J. *Play with a Purpose: A Movement Program for Children.* New York: Harper & Row, 1978. [Based on concept that for children, all physical play activities are a form of movement education, the book is divided into three sections focusing on gymnastics, games, and rhythmic and dance activities; activity suggestions are provided with specific items teachers can look for in evaluating children's progress in developing skills.]

Gilliom, B. *Basic Movement Education for Children: Rationale and Teaching Units.* Reading, MA: Addison-Wesley, 1970. [Introductory portion presents an extensive rationale based on Laban's analysis for teaching movement to young children, while the second part presents actual field-tested lessons with a focus on movement themes and their relationships, specific objectives for children to meet, and a questioning approach within lessons.]

Graham, G.; Holt-Hale, S.; McEwen, T.; and Parker, M. *Children Moving: A Reflective Approach to Teaching Physical Education.* Palo Alto, CA: Mayfield, 1980. [Organized around the section headings of teaching skills, program content, and movement concept and skill theme development, the book is based on Laban's notions about movement but translates these into specific activity progressions, for games in particular.]

Kirchner, G.; Cunningham, J.; and Warrell, E. *Introduction to Movement Education.* Dubuque, IA: Wm. C. Brown Company, Publishers, 1970. [The book contains information concerning purposes, content, and methods of instruction plus nine themes which may be used as concepts, representing a full year's program for young children; there is a game-like quality to the book which challenges children to play along with the teacher; the pictures give good clues as to how children perform.]

Kruger, H.; and Kruger, J. *Movement Education in Physical Education: a Guide to Teaching and Planning.* [An introductory overview of teaching and what children are like, followed by a comprehensive description of Laban's movement concepts; three units aimed at games and sports, gymnastics and body control, and rhythms and dance; an exhaustive description of possible ways to use movement themes in planning lessons.]

Logsdon, B.; Barrett, K.; Broer, M.; McGee, R.; Ammons, M.; Halverson, L.; and Roberton, M. *Physical Education for Children: A Focus on the Teaching Process.* Philadelphia: Lea & Febiger, 1977. [A book strongly oriented toward Laban's analysis of movement, presenting information about basic mechanical principles of motion, curriculum designing, characteristics of the developing child, teaching processes, and ways of evaluating both children and teachers, and detailed descriptions of lesson themes for games, dance, and gymnastics.]

Lowndes, B. *Movement and Creative Drama for Children.* Boston: Play, Inc., 1971. [The book begins with a discussion of what "movement thinking" is and what "creative drama" is, and how both may be used flexibly and imaginatively to get children to "communicate" and learn with enjoyment; uses creative movement and improvisation to help children gain control of their bodies as instruments of expression.]

Mauldon, E.; and Layson, J. *Teaching Gymnastics*. London: Macdonald & Evans, 1965. [A movement concept approach to the teaching of gymnastics, focusing on lesson themes, appropriate design of the apparatus setup in the learning environment, and specific suggestions for teachers about what to do in gymnastics and body control lessons.]

Mauldon, E.; and Redfern, H. *Games Teaching*. London: Macdonald & Evans, 1969. [A movement concept approach to teaching games and sports, emphasizing broad lesson or unit themes for movement related to manipulative skills, progressions for building up to complex skills of ball handling in sports and games, and ways of working with children during lessons to help them think and do instead of being told.]

Monsour, S.; Cohen, M.; and Lindell, P. *Rhythm in Music and Dance for Children*. Belmont, CA: Wadsworth Publishing Company, Inc., 1966. [A very good source for approaches to creative teaching with hints to remember and concepts children should learn.]

Morison, R. *A Movement Approach to Educational Gymnastics*. London: J. M. Dent & Sons Ltd., 1969. [Presents the functional objective action side of movement with the specific intent to develop each individual's movement powers as far as possible, giving a great deal of import to strenuous exercise which stimulates the whole body by using all the muscle groups; the strength of the book lies in its presentation of movement themes based on Laban's analysis of effort into Space, Time, Force, and Flow; although written for an older group, it is applicable to younger children when modified.]

Morris, G. S. D. *How to Change the Games Children Play*. Minneapolis: Burgess, 1976. [An interesting model for helping teachers take a game or activity from any source and modify its rules, strategies, number and roles of players, boundaries, equipment, and other items to vary the game and make it developmentally appropriate for particular groups of children.]

Murray, R. L. *Dance in Elementary Education*. New York: Harper & Row, Publishers, 1975. [A classic reference for the components of a comprehensive dance experience: the skills of dance movement, locomotor, non-locomotor, and combinations; the skills of dance rhythm, pulse, accents, patterns and phrasing; making dances, approaches from imagery and idea, songs, words, music, and learning dances.]

New Games Foundation. *The New Games Book: Play Hard, Play Fair, and Nobody Hurt*. New York: Headlands Press, 1976. [Unusual games within the motto of "play hard, play fair, nobody hurt"; not typical games based on the sports model; some of these are appropriate for young children, many are cooperative ventures minimizing competition and winning.]

Orlick, T. *The Cooperative Sports & Games Book: Challenge Without Competition*. New York: Pantheon Books, 1978. [Cooperative games with an unusual flair, presented without emphasizing competition and with a real sensitivity to the feelings and attitudes of the little people who are the players.]

North, M. *Body Movement for Children: an Introduction to Movement Study and Teaching*. London: Macdonald & Evans Ltd., 1971. [The main purpose of the book is to show how movement can be observed in everyday life, and how it relates to ideas and material for teaching children; it discusses the body as an instrument, action images from nature, group movement, relationships with others, and movement, color, and pattern.]

Peck, J. *Leap to the Sun: Learning through Dynamic Play*. Englewood Cliffs, NJ: Prentice-Hall, Inc., 1979. [Good resource for imaginative ideas on the creative conquest of space and creative movement plays.]

Rohnke, *Cowtails and Cobras: A Guide to Ropes Courses, Initiative Games, and Other Adventure Activities*. Hamilton, MA: Project Adventure, no date. [Billed as "a guide to ropes courses, initiative games, and adventure activities," this book gives suggestions for non-competitive games stressing the emotional and social positive skills children need to learn in addition to their physical skills.]

Russell, J. *Creative Dance in the Primary School*. London: Macdonald & Evans, 1965. [An English approach to the teaching of creative dance for children; begins with Laban's notions of movement concepts and follows this explanation with suggested themes for lessons and possible alternatives for developing each theme; marvelous pictures of children dancing!]

Schurr, E. *Movement Experiences for Children: A Humanistic Approach to Elementary School Physical Education*. Englewood Cliffs, NJ: Prentice-Hall, 1980. [Brief sections discussing the movement curriculum, the teaching process, the characteristics of children, how children learn motor skills, followed by a "traditional" approach to teaching games, gymnastics, and dance activities; includes a wide variety of suggestions for specific games, dances, etc., and is particularly good in presenting leadup games in team and individual sport areas.]

Sinclair, C. B. *Movement of the Young Child Ages Two to Six*. Columbus, OH: Charles E. Merrill Publishing Company, 1973. [The focus is upon the child's developing motor abilities, describing fundamental motor tasks for young children and listing elements and standards for observation and appraisal; the guidelines for helping children are good, as are the suggestions for useful equipment.]

Stanley, S. *Physical Education: A Movement Orientation*. Toronto: McGraw-Hill Company of Canada Limited, 1969. [Good source of material on body and space awareness and relationships, both body parts and people; has some suggestions for themes for lessons for young children which carry out the ideas of concepts and kinds of questions teachers ask with relation to these concepts; kinds of apparatus for the gymnasium are included.]

Torbert, M. *Follow Me: A Handbook of Movement Activities for Children*. Englewood Cliffs, NJ: Prentice-Hall, 1980. [A book full of specific activities under the topics of perceptual and motor development, attention span and concentration, listening skills, release of tension and excessive energy, self-control, development of thinking processes, reinforcement of learned information, social growth, and physical needs; each chapter has suggested activities as well as modifications, comments and suggestions to teachers, and objectives which the activity will help children reach.]

Werner, P. *A Movement Approach to Games for Children.* St. Louis: The C. V. Mosby Company, 1979. [The book contains descriptions of the stages of game playing, concepts involved in games with special emphasis on the process, i.e., making up games, including all factors common to games; contains a discussion of the developmental principles and stages children follow while learning each of the manipulative concepts, exploratory challenges, and guided discovery problems.]

Winters, S.J. *Creative Rhythmic Movement for Children of Elementary School Age.* Dubuque, IA: Wm. C. Brown Company, Publishers, 1975. [Each idea in the book is presented to focus attention on the child and his physical, emotional, mental, and social growth through an awareness of the concepts associated with creative rhythmic movement; lesson plans relate to subject matter presented in the classroom; teaching methods, especially problem-solving, are both clear and useful; the need for equipment is de-emphasized.]

apparatus suggestions

Both small manipulative and large multi-purpose apparatus for young children must be chosen wisely since much of their activity is free and spontaneous play. The apparatus arrangement should be designed to provide facilities for climbing, hanging, balancing, twisting, and turning of the spine, crawling, sliding, and jumping. Teachers who really want to challenge young children, who are far more able than credited, will learn to improvise apparatus setups with *everything* they can find, from volleyball officiating stands to cast-off Olympic apparatus which may not be strong enough for adults but can be used in combination with benches, slides, boxes, and beams for excellent and various provision of the above activities. There are some excellent, but expensive, ready-made products on the market. The authors have used Whittle equipment, particularly, with great satisfaction and success.

Small equipment
    hoops of different sizes and colors
    skipping ropes of different lengths
    long skipping ropes
    elastic ropes
    scooters
    lumi sticks
    bean bags
    dumbells
    tires
    inner tubes, both bicycle and auto
    balls
        Playground: 4'', 5'', 8'', 10'', 13'', 16''
        Plastic balls of different colors
        Footballs
        Soccer balls
        Small basketballs
        Cage balls
        Yarn balls
        Korf balls
        Whiffle balls (various sizes)
    Frisbees

Musical equipment
drum
triangle
tambourine
stick jingles
cymbals
rhythm claves
two tone blocks
rhythm maracas
sleigh bells
wrist bells
castanets

Large equipment
stegel
balance boards, 3'', 6'', 10'' wide
balance beams, various widths
horizontal bar
ladders (vertical and horizontal)
ropes (vertical and horizontal)
cargo net
benches
rings
jumping standards
saw horses 1', 2', 3', 4' high (these can be made very
    easily and painted different colors)
planks, also painted different colors
jungle gym
maze system
mats including a crash pad
hurdles: 4'' x 4'' x 12'' or 18'' or 24'' can be made by
    putting a notch in the top of the 4 x 4 on which a wand
    can rest. When these are painted in different colors
    they are very useful for a variety of activities.

epilogue

Some of the teaching strategies of "movement education", particularly problem-solving and guided discovery, are especially suitable for teaching concepts, and therefore for meeting the objectives of this text.

First there is little ambiguity in a well-stated task or problem. Here's an example for the concept of *weight bearing:* "Find a way to take your weight on your hands." The task is straightforward; the solution immediate. The child either does or does not perform the task. Knowledge of results is immediate and most often child-determined and there is no value judgment involved.

Second the child finds a way to do weight-bearing which is compatible with his developmental level. He may lean forward and momentarily support all weight on both hands or hang from a bar, rope, or ladder (even the youngest child can do this), while others perform cartwheels, roundoffs, or handstands. Accepting different levels of capability and instructing persons with individual differences are extremely important skills for teachers of young children.

Third, as major concepts such as weight-bearing are analyzed into their components (for example, static and dynamic balance, center of gravity over the base of support, width of the base of support, height of the center of gravity), such "operationalizing" permits both teacher and child to focus on the same aspect of movement. Selecting significant cues for moving is one of the skills children must be taught to do if their movement patterns are to improve. Developing a vocabulary of movement terms through learning appropriate labels is an extremely important way of selecting the right cues for children, and certainly underlies the teacher's formulation of tasks and problems.

The next task statement to children following the one above might be, "Find a way to *change* the way you are supporting your weight." Prerequisite to successful completion of a solution is the knowledge of how movement may be changed, and both children and teacher need to know how this occurs. Laban's analysis of movement effort into its components of time, weight, space, and flow provides one way to view the overall curricular decision-making processes teachers use to develop unit plans, lesson plans, and the separate movement tasks within each lesson. The approach from Laban's analysis is particularly significant because it allows all children in the wide developmental age range to be successful, but it is also important because we believe it helps the developing child realize that he *can* change his movement. This concept of personal competence is particularly consonant with the Piagetian notion that development depends on "vigorous interaction with the environment" and that "the child, not the teacher, is the real educator."

Finally if some activities of this text appear redundant, we believe that the one factor distinguishing one activity from another is the FOCUS of the teacher on a particular concept. In other words the same activity may be used at different times as a vehicle for teaching different concepts. And, further, we believe that most of the discipline-based concepts in this text can be placed within the Laban framework of movement analysis. Such connection to this central model appears to reduce the number of specific activities or skills teachers need to know to teach this age range, thus permitting them to apply the concepts to a selected few activities from each of the three broad curricular areas of games, dance, and gymnastics. Hopefully, by relying on Laban's model to provide the conceptual framework, the relationship between learning a specific skill or concept and its use or variations in the contexts of different games, gymnastics, or dances become clearer to both teachers and children.

The paradox of teaching *concepts* to very young children 2½ to 8 years old lies in the fact that, while both teacher and child focus on one concept, the teacher, at least, must become a lateral or divergent thinker in the sense of recognizing many appropriate, successful solutions to the single task presented to children. Thus, instead of teaching one "correct" way to do a forward roll, the whole range of rolling can be explored. It is this writing team's belief that *this* way is the most exciting way to teach — and excitement is contagious!

HELP CHILDREN LEARN THE JOY OF SPORTS

Guidelines For Children's Sports

A new publication designed to encourage the greatest amount of participation in sports under conditions that are safe and enjoyable for all children — boys and girls, handicapped and able-bodied, rich and poor, physically gifted and awkward. The guidelines, developed in cooperation with such groups as the American Academy of Pediatrics and the American Medical Association, are appropriate for all children's sports programs, whether organized by schools, national youth sports agencies, or by regional and local sports organizations.   1979.   48 pp.

BASIC STUFF for K-12 physical educators . . .

(Prices subject to change)

	Regular Price
Series I titles:	
Exercise Physiology (245-26826)	$ 5.95
Kinesiology (245-26828)	$ 5.95
Motor Learning (245-26830)	$ 5.95
Psycho-Social Aspects of Phys. Ed. (245-26832)	$ 5.95
Humanities in Physical Education (245-26834)	$ 5.95
Motor Development (245-26836)	$ 5.95
SIX PACK (all 6 titles in Series I) (245-26838)	$29.95
Series II titles:	
Early Childhood (ages 3-8) (245-26840)	$ 5.95
Childhood (ages 9-12) (245-26842)	$ 5.95
Adolescence (ages 13-18) (245-26844)	$ 5.95
SET OF ALL 3 PUBLICATIONS IN SERIES II (245-26846)	$14.95

ORDER FROM: AAHPERD Publications Sales

P.O. Box 870, Lanham, MD 20801